Good newrn

"...Christina Oxenberg... world." — **Robert F. K**

"Oxenberg depicts in exquisite detail the grotesque side of privilege [Royal Blue]." — **Dominick Dunne**

"Cynics will want to knock it, considering the pedigree it comes from, but that will be tough because Royal Blue's version of a bad and privileged childhood is funny, fetching, and full of gorgeous writing with a deep, tugging undercurrent of melancholy. Its intimate rendering of wealth without cliché is a triumph—imagine Evelyn Waugh rewriting Eloise. For a first novel, what's most remarkable is that there's not a bum sentence in the entire thing." — **Bret Easton Ellis**

"Oxenberg's musings on local culture suggests a style that hints of Tom Wolfe, but with the detached wry and dry observation of Joan Didion, tossed with more than a splash of charming, classy, self-depreciating amusing neurotica that is all her own." — **Dale Launer (author- *My Cousin Vinny* & *Dirty Rotten Scoundrels*)**

"[Royal Blue's] characters are rich and beautiful, and its settings exotic...described with cool detachment and a touch of humour..."
— **The Times (UK)**

"A testament to Oxenberg's powers of survival, [Royal Blue] is, at best, reminiscent of early Francoise Sagan—evocative and surprisingly funny."
— **The Times (UK) Literary Supplement**

"[Royal Blue] is a controlled and vivid account of a sensitive child's survival in the milieu of the fabulously rich.... The catalogue of callousness is shocking." — **The Guardian (UK)**

"[TAXI] Careening along like its subject, the book carries celebrity chatter, historical data, scam stories, and a dictionary of hack-speak....Jump in the backseat for Christina's raucous rides with exhibitionists, Mafia hit men and military tacticians and you'll find the subculture of New York drivers more provocative [than the celebrity passengers]..." — **Vanity Fair**

"...Do These Gloves Make My Ass Look Fat? is sure to make more than a few people laugh out loud." — **East Hampton Independent**

"Darkly funny." — **The Chicago Tribune**

"Oxenberg creates a languid, ferociously beautiful and barbarous world, with an atmosphere reminiscent of that which pervades the work of F. Scott Fitzgerald.... It is an awful story in many ways, but one in which a laugh is never far away." — **The Independent UK, Sunday Review**

"Oxenberg shows herself a master at pulling away comfortable, familiar ground." — **The Independent on Sunday (UK)**

When in Doubt...
Double the Dosage

Sharp, Short, Snappy Stories

For Karen,

Happy reading!

Check out page 73
for help with Rie

♡ Christina
Oxenberg

COPYRIGHT © 2014 BY CHRISTINA OXENBERG

All rights reserved. No part of this book may be reproduced in any form or by any electronic or mechanical means, including information storage and retrieval systems without the prior written permission of the author.

When in Doubt...
Double the Dosage

Sharp, Short, Snappy Stories

by
Christina Oxenberg

Table of Contents

1. Worm Hunt	13
2. Short Break	15
3. House Gecko	17
4. Naked Men	19
5. Fireworks	21
6. Mating	25
7. Captive Audience	27
8. Leader Astray	31
9. Poetic Justice	35
10. Back to Jail	37
11. Orientation	39
12.. Booty	41
13. Wild Life	45
14. Bike Week	47
15. Unit Two	49
16. Not About Alec Baldwin	51
17. Housewarming	53
18. Sick	55
19. Fantasy Fest	57
20. Goldilocks	59
21. Years of Gold	61
22. No Matter	63
23. The Dollhouse	65

24. Enchantment	67
25. Time	69
26. Bird of Paradise	71
27. Life with Pie	73
28. Happy 2013	75
29. Nightbirds	77
30. One Man's Treasure	79
31. Writers on Writers	81
32. Motor Skills	83
33. Perspective	85
34. Winning Moves	87
35. The Traveler	89
36. The Collectors	91
37. Long Road Home	93
38. The King of Key West	95
39. Island Life	99
40. Swine Flu	101
41. Semana Santa	103
42. Yard Sale	105
43. Dreams of Gold	107
44. Party Time	109
45. Studio 54	111
46. Bad Crab	113
47. Saturday Night is Alright	115
48. Night Light	117
49. Saturday Night	119

50. A Strong Hand	121
51. Voice of Ox	123
52. The Boys from Boca	125
53. L.A.R.S.	127
54. Once Bitten	129
55. Mexican Vacation	131
56. When I was Gwyneth Paltrow	133
57. Fight	135
58. No Joke	137
59. Ox & the Pussycat	139
60. Troubled Child	141
61. Yo Bride	143
62. Candace Bushnell Wrecked my Marriage	145
63. Of Mice and Men	147
64. Tales from the Land of Nod	149
65. Speaking of Blood on my hands	151
66. Off Base	153
67. Fantasy Fest 2013	155
68. Parrotheads	157
69. Better than Cake	159
70. Stranger than Fiction	161
71. Things Change	163

Also by

Christina Oxenberg

TAXI

Royal Blue

Do these Gloves Make my Ass Look Fat?

Will Write for Compliments

Life is Short: Read Short Stories

for

YOU, DEAR READER

WORM HUNT

DURING THE New Moon phases in May and June, under cover of darkness, palolo worms are sprung from the coral that populates the seabed off the coast off Key West. Trillions of red and white worms are released from the ocean floor and preprogrammed to swim to an offshore reef, temporarily transforming the liquid they inhabit to an incandescent and colorful froth. No one knows where the hatch will occur, or exactly when, and news of this phenomenon is closely followed, and the coordinates guarded. Fishermen are a notoriously secretive breed. To ask after a location is met with a stony, Out West, or, Bay Side, helpfully narrowing things down to the million nautical miles of the Gulf of Mexico.

Tarpon know when the hatch is going to happen and gather well before it starts. Tarpon are gigantic sardines, shaped like missiles, and the size of skiffs. Tarpon have an oily repulsive flesh, relegating them to sport, rather than steak. Indolent predators usually found submerged near docks, lazily scavenging scraps, however, when the palolo worms sprout from the coral tarpon adopt the personality of crack whores.

Fishermen have scant interest in the worms; they come for the tarpon. A hooked tarpon, interrupted from his orgasmic meal of palolo worms, transforms into a freight train of power and charge, providing a mighty challenge to the angler. Sport fishermen are eager to fish this event because it requires some skill to trick a tarpon in the midst of a worm hunt.

For reasons as yet unexplained by science tarpon lose their minds for the palolo worms. Tarpon travel from all over to engage in this wilding with the worms. They feast on them, they gorge. They roll around and whisk the ocean into a heavy churn, they fling themselves about, frolicking like dolphins. The tarpon devour the tiny worms swimming for their precarious lives. The worms are so small and the fish so big some question the relationship. Some believe the worms are hallucinogenic.

Keen to see these worms and the crazed tarpon I begged a ride from Caloosa, my friend who keeps a boat. It was 10pm. Caloosa is always up for an adventure and soon we were trickling through the harbor half lit from town, chugging around the edge of the piers. Guiding lights in green and red reflect in wobbly ribbons. The air was whitish, dense with moisture, tasting like soda bubbles, making for a mist with which to enshroud the anchored sailboats with their tall masts and wrapped sails, and all of them rocking mildly, a scene stolen from pirate days.

Under a moon like a wafer of beaten gold we gathered speed toward the Atlantic Ocean, port-side passing a forested promontory and the shadows of a civil war Fort. Discouragingly there were a mere handful of crafts on the horizon, spaced sporadically, like fairy lights.

"Not enough boats," Caloosa said, shaking his head.

"Where are the worms?" I implored.

"You missed them," he explained. "Better luck next year."

SHORT BREAK

ONE NIGHT I went hunting for some place to dance.

First stop was Virgilio's, a small club in a narrow alley. Half indoors and with a star-tickler of a kapok tree in the half outdoors side, Virgilio's is a local's choice. Plus, Alex the bartender is always at the ready with my favorite bottled water. But the band was taking a break, so I paid for my water and split.

I stopped in at the fabled Green Parrot, a low slung clapboard structure with rafters hung with beads and bras. The music, while fiercely performed by a meth-fueled violinist, was impossible to dance to. The song finished and the fiddler said, "I'm gonna take a short break. Don't go nowhere."

I went next door to Bobalu's, a bar like a gas station spilling onto the sidewalk, a flapping tarp overhead, a four piece band of lumpy men with straggly hair belting out a marvelous beat. Bobalu's dance floor is a sloping patch of cement and one wrong step can jettison one, but I gave it a go. At the end of the song the band said, "We're going to take a short break, we'll be back in a few days."

I set off down Duval, to the wild end, where stagnant diesel and cigar fumes never dissipate and the lurching crowd seldom disperses. At the corner of Caroline sits a building of three stories, making it a skyscraper. Ground floor is The Bull, second floor is The Whistle, and under the stars is the top floor, with the Garden of Eden. This place is 'clothing optional'. I climbed the stairs and a glance through the entrance revealed titties wobbling and wieners hanging out; meanwhile my bottle of water was confiscated.

The Garden of Eden is an uncovered roof surrounded by a low wall and potted plants, and crowded with dancing bodies. Some clad, some not, many in half-way stages. Two men with blonde afros and dark glasses struggled out of clothes, and then naked, except for bandanas and sunglasses they spun around, helicoptering their tootsie rolls. A big girl in nothing but pink leggings impossibly circumnavigating an ass jutting behind her like the flatbed of a pickup truck, twisted to the techno, entertaining an enormous fellow who watched her, languidly leaning against a potted plant. A torrential rain descended and everyone was kicked out.

The rain was mostly over as I wended to my car. I passed a man with a sack of beer and his friend with a bowler hat and a guitar in a bag on his back. Sack o' Beer said, "I noticed you earlier at Bobalu's, you were dancing up a storm. Have a beer."

Bowler Hat unzipped his guitar and serenaded with songs he claimed he'd composed the day before; they were lovely. Soon we had quite a gathering of others also winding down from the upsurge of the night, and in no particular hurry to go home.

Sack o' Beer offered a hand, "Shall we?"

We danced

.

HOUSE GECKO

IT WAS a windy afternoon and I was securing the house when I saw the mutant lizard. The skies were gray and treetops were swishing, and there was the baby gecko, spying on me from the shadow of my monitor. I had seen him before. He was yellow and rubbery looking, like a section of ginger, except with expressive bulbous eyes. I've watched him scooting across the ceiling and across walls and squeezing beneath window sashes and door jams. It seemed he was looking to get out of the house. I wanted to liberate him, but how? He moved so fast, he evaded my every effort to capture him. I threw towels which landed empty on the floor.

I phoned my friend Caloosa. "Emergency!" I spoke to his voice mail, "A baby gecko is stuck indoors." Caloosa was at home on his houseboat, sage smudging the rooms, spinning the pungent smoke around himself like a ribbon. After a day hosting guests he liked to restore the mojo of his sanctuary. He was swaying to Jazz and sage smudging when the phone rang. He checked the ID. It was that writer chick. He let the call go to voice mail.

The rain descended noisily, bullets strafing dry leaves, rattling heavy palm tree fronds. I dashed about securing wobbly windows, sopping up pools of rainwater that easily entered. The lusty squelching growl of sexed up frogs broke out, groaning in their throaty way, sounding like giants in waterlogged galoshes. I wouldn't have cared except they began to apply themselves to the sliding doors and the windows. Pressing their bodies and bounding away, like fireworks. I watched one frog try to press his vivid green self through a crack in a window, so I sprung over to smack at the glass, and thank heavens he hopped off. Rattled, my eye caught something speeding across the kitchen floor. Suddenly, on automatic, I picked up one foot and planted it directly on whatever was moving, landed squarely on it. I had stomped hard on something pliable and humped. I felt a squishing, and I heard a popping sound. I recoiled, withdrawing my foot, only to see the baby gecko trampled and gooey. His spine was smashed and his tail was split, his legs splayed. But he was still alive. Looking at him I felt sick. He twisted his upper body and turned his head to me, his mouth open, his eyes moist, as if imploring, "Why?" He stared at me, pale eyes beseeching. I was appalled. I knew what I had to do. I raised one foot and crushed him. I felt the torso collapse; felt it give way and flatten, emptying of all hope and aspiration.

After the storm Caloosa sat in his wicker chair on the front deck, watching the rising moon as it glowed through clouds, trapping silver light. He sipped his wine, and returned messages. To the writer chick he said: "That little guy is a House Gecko. They live behind picture frames, and they eat bugs. The House Gecko is your friend."

NAKED MEN

FOR AN excuse to go stare at the naked dancing men I convinced myself, in the name of journalism, I should cover the all male reviews.

These establishments are gathered near the center of Duval, corner of Petronia Street, an oasis within an oasis. Outside one bar drag queens stand tall in massive wigs and platform shoes in which they prance and cheerfully amiably wittily harangue passersby. They are art installations on heels, creativity personified. I was headed for the bar across the way. Five bucks to get in. I paid a bald man in a tank top and thick gold chains. On a wall was a poster, a photo of a man dancing, in profile, in black and white, with heavy shadows playing on a generous rump, and 'Siberian Lynx' beneath. I took a deep breath and pressed against the turnstile of Fate into a multitude of chattering drinking sweating humans. I was in a dim room filled by a stratum of smells, two bars and a stage in the back, and strobe lights clawing through the darkness, and naked men everywhere.

Dancing at the front bar, dangling from a shiny pole, was a lanky white boy with limbs like sticks, and a bandana artfully tied at the top of one slim thigh, holding his equipment in place, rather like a cowboy's holstered gun. He looked no more than nineteen and he had a string of appreciative male patrons in his sway. Farther inside, atop the second bar, a sultry Latin bopped. He had a complexion like coffee and wore only a cowboy hat and underwear with a red patch over the bulge, perhaps to accentuate the obvious. In a frenzy of motion he gyrated near a huddle of females in matching tee shirts, the sure sign of a bachelorette party; they ignored him. Deep in the back, upon the stage the Siberian Lynx was pulsating, his sculpted body thrusting suggestively. He boogied and winked at his mesmerized worshipful clientele. The Lynx had dark hair, pale skin and a red bow for a mouth on an insolent yet striking face. He had his underwear pulled down in the back, so that the elastic waistband was straining beneath the full ripe gluteus. While he danced, occasionally his hands traveled down his etched torso to check the status of the insecure underwear, lest he was asking too much from the elastic. Naturally, as a spectator, it was impossible not to hope the undies would collapse. On my way out I watched aghast as the lanky white boy, in his bandana, had begun to massage himself against a customer's willing thigh, meanwhile they chatted casually.

Later that same night, maybe 4am, I saw the Siberian Lynx in the back of a cab. He was kissing a person with white blond hair. I strained to see, perhaps a lucky customer? Perhaps the lanky white boy? No, it was a female, and surprisingly I recognized her, from the strip club. In the name of journalism, I may have to investigate further.

FIREWORKS

LATE AFTERNOON on July 4th and tourists were massing on the docks at the City Marina to catch the Sunset Fireworks Cruise.

Uncooperatively, on that afternoon, Mother Nature was roughing up the seas, puffing up clouds with a threatening shade and filling the cosmos with ear-splitting thunder. As a consequence of the foul conditions the crew was dispirited; they knew that bad weather acutely affected the culture of tipping. The boat owner did not pay salaries and the mates were expected to earn their keep in tips.

"Will this clear up soon?" the timorous tourists bleated as they were herded onto the boat.

"Of course things will clear up!" replied the mates, trained in damage control and deterring a customer from ever seeking a refund, and handed out life-jackets to a backdrop of cracking lightning.

The boat departed the safety of the piers and chuffed off into an awakening squall. Mates distracted passengers with reams of trivia, statistics and facts and such. Wind raked over the tourists so that they began to shiver and pout and grumble.

Sunset was invisible and any hope of seeing it was swallowed by the whipping gale.

"We want to go back to land!" the tourists had assembled and were attempting a coup.

"The fireworks are going to go off any minute now," mates said soothingly, handing out miniature sodas and small tough squares of cheese and soggy crackers to the mutinous passengers.

"We want to go home!" they clamored, many of them stubbornly refusing the cheese offering. The handful of children aboard stuffed their mouths to the brim with the food.

Thunder detonated overhead, releasing torrents of rain, drenching and silencing the screams of the terrified children. The seawater was dancing and the boat bobbed sickeningly, mustering nausea, until two small children were heaving liberally on their parents. Mates rushed over with rags and a bucket of water, familiar with vomit protocol.

"Look!" mates pointed at a fizzling red firework, flaring into the dark sky and opening up like a flower.

Undaunted by the tempest, Monroe County officials had determined the celebrations were a go. Fireworks had been scheduled, and fireworks there would surely be. The works were dazzling, wondrous colors and lights, and oddly visible despite the thick storm clouds. But the audio of the rockets was muted, enveloped and making for an oddly surreal display. The tourists were briefly hushed, gripping their children in tight embraces, plastic rain protectors snapping in the wind, all faces trained on the pretty lights.

On the return trip to the harbor mates kept their distance from the restive crowd. They knew there would be no gratuities, so they switched out of 'customer' mode, and lit cigarettes and played games on devices. Sure enough, when they docked, tourists scurried away, never looking back, the tip bucket remained echoingly empty.

No one so much as wished the mates a Happy 4th of July. But later that night, in a favorite bar, the mates got piss drunk and picked up some equally lubricated young ladies, and the day was not a total loss.

MATING

WHILE IT'S true the mates did get lucky after the disastrous July 4th fireworks cruise, the collateral damage from that night was a girl named Nelly.

Saturday night, exactly one week later Nelly was primped and awaiting. Nelly was on the early side to arrive at the bar. She knocked back some shots and then bought herself a beer, and a second one, and took up her position. She was waiting for him.

The mates, Boat Boys, you'll spot them in the evenings, traveling in pods. Surging into bars or looping around town in bicycle gangs, hunting for the choicest place to perch, in pursuit of fun.

The band was taking a break when Pirate Bob and his buddies arrived. Somehow Nelly missed him as he got himself a drink and sauntered outside, to linger on the sidewalk, in an optimal position from where he could leisurely catch up with whomever meanwhile dragnet the incoming krill.

This being around midnight, in Key West, the clock had struck play time.

Pirate Bob was lighting a cigarette when Nelly first saw him. With a beer in each hand she made her way over to him, the man of her dreams.

Exhaling a stream of gray smoke it was too late when Pirate Bob's vision crystallized on the blonde in front of him. As the smoke cleared he saw she was tall, slim, and her long blonde hair cascaded in wavy clumps. And then he realized he knew her, and he froze.

She was holding two filled plastic cups of beer. She stared at him as if in a trance. With her narrow face, and her wide dark almond eyes, long lashes casting shadows, her eyelids were half closed, as if perhaps she was deep in thought.

Pirate Bob looked around for an escape route.

"Svor you," Nelly said, and pressed one of her beer cups against him, her tanned arm pecking forward, the beer sloshing to the edge. The liquid splashed onto his shirt.

"No thanks Nelly."

"Thish svor you," she said, again ramming the spare beer at him, so that much of it tipped onto his shorts.

She stared dreamily as meanwhile the object of her affection was gingerly taking steps away, so she followed, and her every thrust was met with a rupture in the matrix. She was grappling, lost in quicksand. She saw a man who to her was perfection. Ever since their one night together she had daydreamed of him, endlessly. She had married him, raised their kids.

Once more she pressed the beer on him, most of what was left in it spilled on his feet.

"Can I call you a cab?" Pirate Bob said.

But she shook her head and with a couple of practiced spins Pirate Bob vanished into the crowd. Later he explained, "Nelly's a good girl, but she is road kill."

CAPTIVE AUDIENCE

KANDY FROM the Key West Library sent me some paperwork I never read, but did sign. Turns out I agreed to visit the ladies at the local lockup. A month before the visit copies of my books were distributed to the inmates.

Driving into the prison compound on Stock Island we passed a small animal farm project, with super-sized Patagonian rodents and hundred year old turtles and garishly plumaged ducks, all rescues and now roaming freely. We passed a block of cement with no open windows, the Juvenile Detention building, and adjoining this, another three story block of cement, lodging the women.

Indoors is drab cinderblock walls and disinfectant and flat lighting. A guard, young with sly eyes, came with name tags, to pin to our clothes.

From a panel on the wall he opened a heavily reinforced door. We passed a sign reading 'no weapons beyond this point', which I thought was a grand idea. And then there you are, in a main hall, a room like the inside of a gigantic turret, open plan with high ceilings and a metal stairwell joining a second tier circumnavigated with cell doors, just like on TV. Some doors were open, revealing bland spaces with cots and metal toilets. The main room has tables and chairs and everywhere were women, all dressed in blue baggy scrubs, observing our entrance. Kandy recognized some faces and some called out hellos. The guard led us to a room off to one side, with desks.

Ladies streamed in and filled the desks. I clung to a back wall and tried to appear calm. Some had my books on their desk tops, some had bibles.

With everyone seated Kandy introduced me. I had not prepared to lecture. Had I thought I was attending a tea party, now that I thought about it I had no clue.

I opened by saying I had another book Kandy had not been allowed to distribute as the prison authorities had banned it. Instantly quiet descended and all eyes were trained on me, accompanied with wide grins, and the ice was broken.

Encouraged, I launched into the chronology of my life story, familiar ground, except I discovered I was continually editing. For example, I always describe boarding school as being exactly like jail, but here I stopped and looked around, and realized I didn't want to say that. Equally I didn't want to employ words or concepts with negative overtones, like kill, death, hate, revenge, etc… words I regularly use in my chronic bombast. I tried not to curse, not to blaspheme, and ended up a little tongue-tied.

At the end of it all the ladies proffered their notebooks and stubby pencils and I signed my name and drew hearts beneath. Some of us hugged. Someone asked me to return.

"Shall I give you an assignment?" I proposed.

"Yes!" they replied.

Which is when I had a flash of genius; these ladies could be writing my blog for me! "Write five hundred words on anything you like." I said excitedly, as I realized how I could exploit this factory filled with willing apprentices ready to churn out copy.

I have benevolent dictator blood coursing through my veins, and the captive audience was exhilarating. I can't wait to go back to jail.

LEADER ASTRAY

I ATTENDED fourteen schools in all, but the one I loathed the most was very hard to leave. Trust me, I tried everything. This was a windswept Dickensian nightmare on the south coast of England.

In the evenings, after Matron had performed her rounds, checking to see we were all in bed, it was time to play. My best friend Gia was fearless and up for anything, her only fear was spiders.

After 'lights out' Gia and I would hustle fellow miscreants and I would lead us out onto the Downs and the White Cliffs of Dover. If we happened across a construction site we would set about removing tools and chucking them about. We dragged planks and anything not bolted down and hurled them over the cliffs.

As dawn peaked, after a night's ransacking, we would return to the school, breaking back in how we had escaped, through the kitchen window.

One time, upon re-entry, we heard the sounds of Matron. There were eight of us on that particular excursion and we had just crawled in through the window. Matron was calling out names.

Gia and I scrabbled to the safety of the larder, and tucked ourselves beneath a shelf holding a large bowl of white flour. Matron was hollering. Next we heard the heavy kitchen door swing open, clattering against the wall.

Which is exactly when I saw it, at the lip of the shelf above my head, a blob shimmering, scratching at the air.

Matron banged around the kitchen. "You're in for it now!" she barked.

The glistening blob tumbled an inch. My heart stopped when I realized it was a spider repelling on his shiny cord. Gia would go mad. The spider dropped another inch and swung at eye level.

I heard the swinging kitchen door slamming against the wall and Matron was gone.

But just then Gia saw the spider as he was descending in jerks, and she jolted upright, knocking the shelf, tipping the bowl of flour so that it exploded and rained down, white lava dust.

"Who's that?" Matron shrieked.

Gia bolted, with me in hot pursuit. As Matron re-entered the kitchen, we fled out the other door, to the main hall and on to the dining room.

Matron was close behind, yelling, "Stop! I can see you!"

We dashed to the far end of the dining room and tucked ourselves behind velvet curtains, panting heavily. And there we prayed for a miracle.

"I can see your fingerprints all over the curtains!" Matron was saying, "Come out now!"

We were captured, and punished. When I was hauled in front of the headmaster, with Matron standing beside him looking priggish,

I was warned, "Any more trouble out of you Oxenberg and you will be expelled."

I was dejected. I had tried everything, had given them my best material. I was out of ideas. This gulag lasted another few years, and when at last I left, most of the staff cheered.

POETIC JUSTICE

WHEN I arrived at the boarding school on the south coast of England I despised it on sight. The building was all redbrick and turrets and wrapped in fog with an incessant wind blustering against windowsills and slamming doors. Inside was dark and infused with vinegar and boiled cabbage.

Luckily I was placed in a dormitory with a girl named Gia, and we became friends. For one thing, she too was an insomniac, and for another we shared grand plans and schemes. Chattering all throughout the nights, covering topics revealing a desire for adventure and excitement, we giggled in between the snores of others, and frequently Matron overheard us and stormed in, caterwauling for "Silence!"

"Don't be cross!" we'd plead, "We thought we saw a ghost!" And Matron would over-boil, as we hoped she would, and her dentures would fly from her mouth, and we would hide beneath bed sheets, crumpled laughing.

Official meals were inedible, for example Wednesday's tomato soup was always filled with flies plying the surface with the backstroke, or Friday dinner, called bubble and squeak, essentially fried leftovers from the entire week. Consequently we were always hungry and we became obsessed with food. Most nights we raided the kitchen where we stuffed on sandwiches of bread and butter and sugar. We were naughty, no doubt about it, but Gia and I were only ten years old.

By the spring semester Gia and I were moved to different dormitories. But there was only a thin wall between our new locations, and with the help of spoons we dug a hole in the wall, and taped up photographs to conceal the opening. As the weather improved, to help fill the dull night hours, we let ourselves out the kitchen window off to vandalize the Sussex Downs. We were frequently caught, and one time Gia was "sent home in disgrace." I seethed with envy.

Nearing the end of the summer semester, one afternoon, I knocked at the headmaster's door. I thought I had assembled classmates into a united front, we were going to strike, but when the time came nobody else showed up. The Headmaster's office was yellow chintz and cozy and smelled of sugar; I wanted to lick the air.

"Yes?" the Headmaster said, tiny spectacles on a gray face, staring out the window, at fog. I delivered my demands, and that was the end of that.

I have always referred to this boarding school as a 'prison', however, compared to the real thing I will concede I was exaggerating. Which reminds me, I'm returning to the Federal Penitentiary tomorrow to see what the ladies have produced in the way of creative writing.

The irony is not lost on me what a deplorable student I was and the notion that I could ever be a teacher, of English no less, would not have seemed remotely plausible all those years ago. I shall keep my delinquent past to myself as I attempt to motivate my students.

BACK TO JAIL

LAST MONDAY evening I paid my second visit to the ladies in the County lockup. I was saying hello to faces I recognized as twenty of us converged in the class room, dragging the chairs and desks into a circle. Gradually I noticed there were new faces in the room. One new face in particular caught my attention, a tall slim lady with a buzz cut. She definitely was not here last time and yet something about her looked familiar. We all sat down and the lady caught me staring at her and she stared back intently, and then, slowly, her face creased into a frown. I knew I should look away but then her wide blue eyes were popping, and she silently mouthed, "You?"

It was Crystal! Astonished, I nodded my head, and could not suppress a smile. She looked mortified.

"In the interest of full disclosure," I began, gesturing across the room, "Crystal and I are friends." Instantly, all eyes were on Crystal who lowered her eyes and re-crossed her long legs. I pushed on. "Crystal gave me one of the best nights of my life." The ladies went mad, cheering and applauding, smacking desktops.

"Crystal and I met one night in an alley behind Schooner Wharf," I said, and I would have described Crystal's outfit of bald head, silver spandex leggings and a black bra, but as I spoke I watched her and she looked decidedly queasy with eyes downcast and chewing on her lip. Her discomfort was palpable so I modulated our history, sanitizing it to a tale of inspiration and joy. I told how Crystal put a smile on the faces of everyone we passed. What I left out was how she placed that smile, which was by pulling down her bra, and with nipples shaped like bullets stuffing them into the mouths of passersby, including men and women and the wheelchair bound. Shrieks followed our progress along Duval Street. Crystal grabbed the crotches of club bouncers, huge fierce men, reducing them to giggles, as they pushed her off, affectionately scolding, "You can't do that!" Crystal grabbed the crotches of old men, "Oh you good girl. Come back here!" the old men squeaked, thrilled, as Crystal was twirling off and away, with me in pursuit bent over from laughing. At some point she confided, "I just don't want to end up back in jail."

But that is Crystal's story to tell, and her secrets are safe with me. She exhaled with relief as I moved the focus off of her.

Many of the ladies had prepared stories to read. Each story was distinctly different; some were raw with feeling, while others were funny, some rhymed, one was sung as a rap song. And in their own way they were all good. One day soon when permission is granted, I plan to post them on my website.

At the end of it all I gave them a second assignment. Crystal refused it, saying, "I'll be out before you get back here. We'll go for martinis." And that will be another story.

ORIENTATION

IN ORDER for me to regularly visit the jail I had to pass a background check, sign and initial paperwork and partake of 'Volunteer Orientation', a meeting where the prison rules and regulations were explained.

I arrived early one afternoon and waited in a main lobby and watched flustered kin squabbling over bail money while other visitors lined up at the metal detector, patted down by bored-looking officers.

A door in the corner of the big room bursts open. "Anyone for Orientation?" said a tiny lady. I put up my hand and hustled for the open door.

Tiny steered us through an administrative bullpen to a conference room with a grand view of the Gulf of Mexico. Tiny was cheerful, bordering ecstatic. Awaiting us in the conference room was her partner, Tall, who emanated a steely serenity. Tall runs a work release program. She takes very personally the successes and failures of her 'babies' as she fondly calls them, and she smiled and the tough exterior briefly softened.

"The Lord is always with you," Tall said. "That's what I tell all my babies."

"Amen!" Tiny cheered, throwing her head back and closing her eyes.

Tiny drew the blinds and ran a video. Fifteen minutes of actors swishing around a jail setting. We followed the story of a volunteer teacher as she sauntered about dispensing bon-mots and seemed to be having a glorious time. Officers and guards appeared placid; meanwhile hairy tattooed felons meowed with appreciation. Gentle music accompanied the part about how to respond if security is threatened. Beaming as she calmly sequestered herself into a bulletproof cell the raconteur-teacher implored, keep calm and stay out of the way.

After the video, Tiny distributed pamphlets which she slid to Tall who pushed them toward me. Tiny led us through the printed matter, taking time to digress and offer examples to help illustrate the need for the rules. Why exactly I was not permitted to show my breasts (could incite a riot), or toes (one time a volunteer fell in a crack and broke her foot and blamed her flip-flops), and so forth.

"Never make promises you can't keep!" Tiny guffawed. "They will try you!"

"Don't get fooled," Tall interjected. "Anything they ask just say you'll bring it up with the Director. That usually puts an end to it. I can tell what's up in three sentences. They will try to con you. They're not evil. Not all of them. Mostly they are a bunch of fruit loops." "Amen!" Tiny agreed.

At the end of the brochure Tiny swiftly and dismissively dealt with how to respond should I be taken hostage. "This has never happened," Tiny was quick to add, "But if it does and you can't run away just agree to everything. Do not negotiate or bargain. Best is don't talk. Just sit quiet and wait for help to arrive."

Tall added, "Just sit quiet, and pray."

Amen

BOOTY

THE STORMS of Key West, historically speaking, were a time of great booty. A storm might take down a galleon stuffed to the gills with treasure. Wreckers and pirates and all manner of opportunists only had to sit back and wait, and let nature do her thing. The benefactors of the plunder made a killing and in its heyday Key West was the wealthiest city in America.

All week there has been unrest as locals took seriously the weather reports of hurricane warnings. Friends urged: get supplies, get prepared. I've heard about these storms and I'm perversely excited to see what all the fuss is about. But just in case, off I went to purchase the batteries, flashlights, crackers, water and anti-looter spray I'm assured I will need. The wind is whipping the tops of trees, and the temperature has dropped from a previous oppressive humidity, I can't help liking the change. Locals are boarding up homes and store fronts, plywood nailed over doors and windows, sandbags tilt against doorways. Pickup trucks cart away newspaper vending machines, even the painted bollard marking the Southernmost Point is attended to, mysteriously wrapped in cellophane.

On my way to buy supplies, on Truman Avenue, I got stuck in traffic, right outside the pawn shop, the one with the false leg in the window. Traffic was clogged on account of a slow moving funeral procession preceded by a marching band, and taking its sweet time to get out of my way. I could see this was going to be slow, so I parked and slipped into the pawn shop. Bells warbled when I pushed open the glass door. The room was cavernous yet cluttered with shelves to the ceiling, all weighed down with forlorn objects. Half busted overhead lights, swinging from chains vied with daylight insinuating itself through the gloom. The air was the color of dust, and the atmosphere was one of time passing, of dreams decaying.

"Welcome! Let me know if I can show you anything." A man I had not noticed called out.

I laughed, "I'm just looking, thanks."

My eyes traveled swiftly over the fingerprint-smudged glass casements. Chunky ugly jewelry sat on beds of black velvet, and I scanned it all in milliseconds. On account of the ramifications of my background as something of a Serbian princess I am trained to recognize quality. So when I saw the green rock my attention was galvanized.

Equally attuned was the shopkeeper, he knew the look in my eyes.

"Find something?" he asked, bustling over.

"Um, yes, may I see this green rock?"

"That's an emerald," he said, opening the casement. "It's from the Atocha."

"Really?" I was dubious.

"It's worth sixty grand. You can have it for thirty," he said, and retrieved the jewel. It caught the light and it sang to me.

"May I touch it?" I said, entranced.

"Carefully," he said and placed it on the glass top.

With the tips of my fingers I took the barrel shaped gem, gently fingering its smooth cut sides. I could feel the heft of its provenance.

"Thank you," I said, exhaling like a snorting horse, as I reluctantly returned it. "That was an experience!"

Perhaps the storm will wash up booty from the deep blue sea.

WILD LIFE

THE PERILS of south Florida are being neatly dispatched. First, there was the life threatening weather that never materialized and second, Mr. Snake vanished. I noticed he had not appeared in quite some time, and in the loosest sense I missed him, worried what had become of him.

All summer long, everywhere I looked, my eye was tricked by shade, by a section of garden hose, by a benign frond, and I jumped in place and visualized the quick moving beast looping up my bare legs, puncturing my jugular with a well placed fang. I could feel him on me in every swish of innocent leaves. I was hyper aware of his not coming around because for a time I was waiting for him, like an assassin, ready to implement whatever permanent damage I could muster.

I had petitioned everyone I know for ways to handle this intruder. Smack it with a shovel, make friends with it, feed it, ignore it, give it a name, were just some of the extraordinarily lame suggestions flung my way. One friend counseled, "Don't be such a weenie! It's a rat snake, they eat rats. Just don't step on it." Reluctantly, and fully creeped out, I cleared the heaps of fallen leaves and the mounds of squishy balls that continually thunder down from a sweet almond tree. The best suggestion came from my mother, HRH Princess Elizabeth Karageorgevic, who spent a good portion of her childhood in Kenya. "Easy! Get a mongoose," she advised. "I had a pet mongoose when I was a child, and they love to eat snakes."

I searched for a place to purchase a mongoose, but I was unsuccessful, and gradually as the months accrued I couldn't help but notice Mr. Snake was not around. Did he somehow know of my nefarious intentions? Until recently, one hot afternoon, I saw him in the front yard sliding hesitantly alongside the scruffy path to the street. I froze and watched as he poked slowly forward, where the burned grass is sparse and the ground is dry and there he was, a length of diamond patterned oily blackness starkly contrasted against the desiccated landscape. And then he noticed me, and he stopped moving. I had no desire to get any closer than was necessary. It was a standoff.

Then, bafflingly, Mr. Snake stuck his small head beneath a leaf, keeping the rest of himself perfectly still.

"That's all you've got?" I just stared at him. I was shocked. "Thousands of years of evolution and that's your selfdefense mode?" I laughed and I stamped my foot. "Now off you go!" and thank heavens he swished away.

So the summer ends, the snake lives, and all is well in the Florida Keys.

BIKE WEEK

FLORIDA'S SOUTHERNMOST Key had been overrun by bikers. It is Bike Week, and for three days and nights I have heard the growling rumble of the motorcycles as they headed south, to downtown Key West. I had to go look. Lined up along both sides of Duval Street were rockets and choppers of all colors and engineering-defying shapes, and all around milled men in jeans and chunky boots and leather waistcoats with patches declaring allegiance to this or that motorcycle club. A great deal of visible skin was festooned with tattoo art. And everywhere I looked there was a great deal of skin on display. Mostly from the biker molls, many of whom had stopped in at the 'body paint' booth of a maestro, a ponytailed man wielding a spray gun. The molls fearlessly whipped off their tops and had their chests painted with trompe l'oeil, so that once more they appeared dressed, until a breast slung into profile, and the give away was a cheeky nipple.

It was the middle of the afternoon and while no doubt everyone was working on their drunk as best they could, and despite the embellished breasts, the mood was more 'family' than 'hell's angels'. Some excellent music hauled me indoors momentarily and I ventured into Sloppy Joe's, where framed photos of Ernest Hemingway loom all over the walls. In one, looking so very correct and unimpeachable in a roll neck fisherman's sweater and cap, and a pipe in his mouth. A rock and roll band dominated the raised stage, bouncers in orange teeshirts filled every crevice, watching closely, never smiling, on high alert. The band was four men with blow-dried hair and shirts open to the navel, jeans that split at the ankle, decorated with diamanté studs, boots of suede with heels covered in crushed sparkly gems. As they thrummed their guitars they would smile at one another and that's when I saw the lines, the creases around their mouths, lines flaring at the edges of their eyes. They were fabulous and when they fired up the redneck anthem of Sweet Home Alabama I had to throw myself into a white girl jig. Because, really, how could I not? Plus there was a thick crowd of dancers to hide within. Except someone brushed me, transferring disgusting gobs of warm sweat onto my exposed arm. I tried not to retch.

Then an incredible noise overwhelmed the puny sound system of Sloppy Joe's, throbbing reverberations like perhaps a space ship was landing. The band courageously played on, but they could not be heard so out I went back to the action on Duval Street. Here I discovered a massive Harley Davidson in black and glitter, fully reconfigured to mimic a discotheque. Every possible compartment including gargantuan saddle bags were cleverly concealed speakers. The decibel level was ear shattering. A friend recognized the tune, it was a ditty called, 'Bitch! Get Out of My Way', by the musical master Ludacris.

And a good time was had by all.

UNIT TWO

DISASTROUSLY, THE landlord is upping my rent by a fortune. He claims he has a valid airtight excuse for this outrageousness. I disagree.

Initially, I clung to the idea of staying, and to that end I wrote him a scorcher of a letter. Thankfully, I sent this to someone else. Her advice was to sleep on it. Sure enough, the next morning, in the gentle light of day, I trashed the rant, realizing it's simply time to move on.

Bubbling with resentment I fired up Craigslist. Sighing loudly I clicked on 'for rent' and drifted across the listings, making notes and phone calls. The response was invariably, 'Sorry, I rented the place yesterday'.

I recognized many of the rentals from last year's quest. I remembered the scam ads, like the one promising a luxury Key West address which in reality is a broken down mobile home many islands northward up the chain. I shuddered at the flashback of a place called an 'efficiency', a somber cell barely large enough for a change of mind.

One place was so cheap I was tantalized. The woman on the phone begged me not to visit before the caretakers were done with repairs. I lied heartily and promised I would not. Meanwhile, still on my cell phone, I was backing out of my driveway and heading over. I parked out front of a sprawling ramshackle clapboard building of a couple of floors, and balconies hung with towels, clearly once a stately mansion, long ago carved into a warren of dwellings, with doorways like stable doors. Many layers of paint flaked the sides like shingles. A sagging porch ran all the way around, and beside each front door were clusters of plastic chairs, some knocked over.

The door to Unit Two was open and I cautiously entered, stepping over orange cables and around workers' buckets and rusty saws. Unit Two was a single room with raw floors. I tried to picture myself living there. Due to the incredibly low rent I wanted to find a way to like the place. The image remained hazy.

Sauntering around the grounds, I carefully picked my way over tumbled discarded junk and fleeing cats. And that's when I saw some potential neighbors, chatting amiably. One was a whisper-slim old man, leaning on a rake. The other was naked except for sagging shorts that vanished beneath a vast belly. I tried not to stare, aghast. Behind my sunglasses I felt suitably invisible, slowing my gait as I passed them, keen to pick up the scent of their exchange.

Old man: What do you do?

Fat belly: I'm a musician

Old man: Oh yeah, where do you play?

Fat belly: At home, in my living room

They wobbled with laughter, and clinked beer cans.

I was considering slitting my wrists when friends called, and offered a quiet space in their new and huge and empty house. Thank you, I said accepting.

Time to go.

NOT ABOUT ALEC BALDWIN

I WAS scheduled to get on a plane yesterday, for New York City. I was expected for dinner with a Greek tycoon, a movie producer and the actor Alec Baldwin.

All day I kept looking at the time, keeping pace with what needed doing. I should pack now, I thought and I took some teeshirts off hangers and placed them on a chair. I should buy that ticket now, I thought next. But it was not yet noon and my flight was at four o'clock, so I went for a bike ride, along the esplanade with the ravishing view of the ocean.

On my ride I passed a man holding a slim chain, and a few paces behind him, at the other end of the chain, rumbling along, a monkey wearing a bowler hat. A howler monkey maybe, with a long tail snapping around like a flag in the breeze.

I was hot and the ocean looked so inviting so I locked my bike, and rushed into the waves. I was diving into the warm water, swimming off claustrophobic visions of airports, and the barefoot herding alongside conveyor belts of possessions rattling in tubs. In a burst I swam fast and then I dove down to the ocean floor, spinning myself like a hedonistic torpedo.

With some nervous energy sluiced, I floated in the surf, bobbing like drift wood. I watched a man sprinting from the palm tree line, zig zagging across the sand like he was avoiding enemy fire, his long hair flying, and as he neared the water he thrust upward into the air, twisting his body so that his back hit the waves, all of him sinking under the bubbling navy froth.

Another man, dripping with seagrass, emerged from the deep, his mask pushed up. All of him slamming through the resistant water, dragging his legs until he was stepping onto the sand, picking up his oversized black rubber fins in clumsy steps. In one hand he clutched a rod almost as long as the man was tall. At one end of the pole a large pink shape flapped. Some kind of fish. Before he could drop it into a chest of ice a gaggle of children appeared from nowhere, leaning on one another in their curiosity to see the enormous catch.

When I got back home I saw the time, it was four o'clock, and presumably the plane was locked up tight, and racing down the runway, and taking off, without me. I felt a bit bad. Later, when a full moon took center stage in an onyx sky, my phone began to sound. It was my dinner companions, no doubt curious as to my whereabouts.

Incapable of explaining my behavior, I turned the ringer off and ventured downtown. Ending up in a bar where I became transfixed by a band rocking Hendrix. I danced all night, and only occasionally wondered what Alec would be talking about at that dinner party in New York City.

HOUSE WARMING

I AM on the brink of moving again and meditating on what to pack and what to toss out. What to do with my most prized possession?

My glorious hammock; it was originally a hot brown, with whipped cream colored pillows that lace to poles stretching it to a welcoming rectangle, a chocolate bathtub, in which to heave oneself and contemplate the meaning of life while nuzzling the sweet warm breezes.

The tropics are hard on a fabric, even one as robust as woven rope. After a full year splayed under a fire-eating sun the color has faded, even the cream pillows are blotchy and pocked with mashed sugar ants. However, the greatest damage was inflicted by the iguana who inhabits the sweet almond tree.

All year the iguana has, in moments of privacy, slung himself from the branches, landing in my hammock and clawing at the ropes, and after steadying himself, lurching off into the garden, possibly just for the fun of it. He plods awkwardly through the gigantic grass, stomping along, his whiplike tongue flickering out. For terrain mode he styles himself in lime green, with his tapering tail in alternating moss and pebble. From behind a glass door I watched him, noticed how even the geckos bound out of his way, like a liquid splash. Clearly, they do not see the fruit eater as any kind of ally. I slid the glass door open and instantly the iguana heard me and raised himself into tank mode and picked up speed and rumbled off toward the tree, and then he lanced his long claws into the tree trunk, and hoisted himself vertical. I dashed over to where he was and caught site of a glimpse of him as he shimmied into where the branches were thick, saw the last of his mottled tail, vanishing into a curtain of broad leaves. Which is when I heard a noise I recognized. All year, late at night I've heard this disquietingly loud rustling, like perhaps a trillion newspapers being flapped simultaneously. At last now I know definitively such is the sound of a large and startled and bolting iguana.

One time I witnessed something so vile I remain a little traumatized. I was prone in the hammock when above me, straddling a branch, was the iguana. It took me a moment to be sure it was he, camouflaged as he was, exactly mimicking the colors of the branch. It appeared his eyes were closed. Next, all of him flexed, and then, hideously, he began to emit an endless tube of dark substance, followed by an impressive fountain arc, landing all over me. Instantly, I remembered many times swinging in the hammock, and thanking the heavens for my good fortune, when I had felt 'rain drops'.

The iguana will no doubt be pleased to see me gone, moving on. I'll be foisting the hammock on my new hosts. I'll tell them it is a 'housewarming' gift.

SICK

LAST YEAR I abused my buddy Carlos, a much overworked New Yorker with a mostly uninhabited upper east side penthouse, and a Swedish car in a garage. I commandeered his guest room for a few weeks, and helped myself to the Swedish vehicle, without permission, and got caught.

So it was fitting that when he was invited to a conference in Palm Beach, he would rent a car and visit me here in groovy Key West, if only for revenge.

He could not find my house so I met him in the parking lot of the Waffle House. Black hair, black sunglasses, dark red skin, sitting in a silver convertible. He was staring forward, smoking a cigarette. I walked up from behind him and saw, on the passenger seat, a styrofoam of half-devoured waffles and syrup and sausages dying under the hot sun.

"Welcome!" I said.

"Fuck, that's a long drive," Carlos said, "I need a drink." As he looked up at me, his broad back shuddered and he began to bellow with a cough like a braying donkey. One hand slammed against his open, retching mouth, catching phlegm and spume.

I showed him around but after many hours driving in the blistering sunshine, and a solid evening of liquids, by midnight Carlos was sweating and slurring. And with his infernal cough still exploding like a fuming coal train I took him home and pushed him into the guest room.

Warning: the following material may be offensive to frailer readers:

That is when I heard the thump. It was a huge noise. Like perhaps a door had come off its hinges and shattered on the ground. Or perhaps my houseguest was dead.

I rushed to the door of the guest room, and there I stopped, with my hand levitating above the brass handle and I hesitated, and wondered what to do. My inclination was to walk away and pretend I had not heard the thump. But I could not so, reluctantly, I returned to the door, and listened for clues. Nothing. I rested my hand on the door handle and as I pressed and slowly opened the door, with my free hand I was gently knocking, and saying, "Hey, everything OK in there?"

But right away Carlos was screaming, "Don't come in! Close the door!"

I slammed the door, and began yelling, "I didn't see anything!" But I had seen. I had seen everything. This is what I saw:

In the darkened guest room, back lit with moonlight streaming in the window, I saw an enfeebled and crumpled naked body kneeling on a tile floor that shone like a lake, like a luminescent puddle, flecked with bits. I was puzzling as to the nature of the wetness when, as I shut the door, a smell like acid had escaped and was busy corroding the inside of my throat.

And for a parting gift Carlos bequeathed his pox

.

FANTASY FEST

FANTASY FEST has come and gone. Since arriving here a year ago I have heard of this spectacle from the locals, but had yet to witness it myself.

Fantasy Fest is the entire week before Halloween when the bulk of Key West participates in a carnival of craziness. Duval Street is blocked off for pedestrians, and each night is dedicated to a theme of dress, one night all red, another night togas, and so on, the madness building to a crescendo by Saturday night with a parade of floats. This annual freak-out is when fifty-thousand out-of-towners descend upon this tiny coral island and partake in the nuttiness.

Naturally, I went to look and for the most part I was too astonished to remember to raise my camera. Mostly I walked about with my mouth agape, busting with spontaneous giggles at the outlandish sights. Such as the enormous naked muscular man wearing only work boots and a 'hammock' for his equipment and a black mask with a closed zipper at the mouth. Many costumes were impressively detailed, most were scant and provided a voyeur's delight. Mostly what I saw were breasts, cleverly painted with a thick shellack and reconfigured to a lion's face or draped fabric and so on as far as the imagination can go. Many women were completely nude with appliqué hearts pressed on at the coochie, presumably in a salute to modesty. But I feared for those older gals with pendulous pancake breasts, with nipples getting ensnared in belt buckles. I can say definitively that old adage about the beauty of the female body, is not really the case after all. No, that adage only applies to the young female body. Turns out older women are like men, better looking dressed.

One couple, a tall Caucasian man dressed as a spiky ball tethered to a tall African American man dressed in nothing much beyond a chain wrapped around himself. The two danced in the middle of the street. "He's all ball!" Chain declared conspiratorially and he flogged at his mate, and they both laughed and kept on dancing.

A section of parking lot had been closed off with black-out material and I pressed myself against it so as to see within. It was a thousand people dressed in S&M gear, and one enormous naked man kneeling up on a stage, his head and hands locked in a 'stocks' and a very tall man in leather and zips whipping the hell out of his exposed buttocks.

After a week of such scenes I still feel all of me thrumming, profoundly stunned, like perhaps I had been shot in the face and splattered with impressions and noises, music and words and my own thoughts popping like bursting bubbles. After a week of slopping through sticky lakes of spilled beer and being poked in the ear with an angel's wing I must revert to daytime and pretty vistas of sunshine and white balance my tiny mind.

GOLDILOCKS

I HAVE Brazilian sounds on the radio. I've been packing for days and I'm busy with the movers, taking my furniture to my next stop, a guest room like a Polynesian hut on the roof of a friend's new house, still something of a construction site. You have to see it to believe it.

As I pack and tape and move the boxes around, some unopened since the last move from Long Island, I'm swaying about to the Samba and the Bossa Nova, enjoying myself and ready for the next adventure, ready for a change of scenery without crossing the border of the Conch Republic.

I dance around saying good bye to the house and thank you for the shelter, but no offense I won't miss you much, maybe the outdoor shower, and the garden and its sense of privacy, however false, after all, with my own eyes I saw the neighbor, quite still on a top step of the next door building, in his checked chef pants, observing me while I did yoga in the garden, and not only once. He was rather sexy, so I didn't entirely mind, but still.

And once again Murphy's Law doffs his hat. After a full year of bucking, the sliding screen door from the kitchen into the garden, well suddenly now, the instant before I'm moving out, it is gliding back and forth like an ice skater, easily grabbing a track it has been blind to, since the day I moved in. And now it moves like it's been oiled, oiled by Murphy that dastardly clown. And another touch with a chair that is turned around, ready for the truck and now I see it was how it should have been all along, exactly perfectly out of the way yet with a commanding view of all, garden and sunset included. This is mildly annoying because all year I've swiveled this chair hither and yon in the search of the perfect position, and now, by accident I've found it. Touché Murphy, what can I say?

Poised to follow my stuff to the roof dwelling I discover a certain hombre has beat me to it. Goldilocks, we'll call him, has come from afar, with wobbly credentials as a master carpenter, and worse, impersonating an opera singer, because he knows the hosts' worship the medium. My hosts tell me Goldilocks is only staying a few days, to asses the job he will return to complete. Sacré Bleu, I splutter, I cannot share my bowl of porridge, or God forbid, a bathroom, not even for a matter of days and now I am lost in space, I am the abandoned luggage on the airport carrousel, rocking around on the conveyor belt of life.

Swaddled as I am by good fortune, another friend took me in and now I am pitched up in an empty mansion where I wallow in super deluxe and wait for Goldilocks to vacate my space. But I'm in no hurry.

YEARS OF GOLD

BACK TO the Judo competition in Miami, this time the senior gentlemen. In the warmup room men in blue or white pajamas grappled in pairs, or sat on the mats, stretching. One man was upside down and rolling on his head. Traces of body odor coast the air, or was that the scent of controlled fear, all of it tempered by a supersonic A/C.

There were men with hunchbacks, with wiry comb-overs, mustaches were grey. Men with wounds, pink blemishes on bald heads. The oldies tussled and soon they were rosy cheeked. Some sported reading glasses on speckled hairless pates. Everywhere there were braces on legs and elbows, even heavy shin guards beneath the thick regulation pajama bottoms.

Taki, legendary columnist and all of 76 years old, was in there with Brian, his teammate, and today his coach. Brian massaged Taki's shoulders. Taki grabbed Brian by the collar and threw him to the ground. He repeated this move several times, one time landing on Brian.

With no one else his age to fight Taki was dropped down into a younger category. Soon he discovered his opponent was a very experienced giant. It was the Hollywood actor Bo Svenson, of Walking Tall. Turned out Bo had signed up for the mete, traveled from California and yet never weighed in, and up until the very last second he was dithering. When Bo met with Taki, being seven years his junior, looking down from almost a foot more in height, and at least forty pounds more in weight, and claiming that his ears were fragile from recent surgery to pin them back, he declared, "I'll fight you."

The fight started and in an instant Taki was yanked to the mat by Goliath. It seemed to be over before it began. I was terrified for my friend as he was obviously about to be killed.

Taki was on the floor. Brian was on the sidelines, yelling, "Move your leg!" And Taki did, and it released him from Bo's sure grip. Brian yelled, "Pin him!" And Taki, now laying over Bo and looking extremely serious as he transformed into a wall of arms and elbows somehow constrained the enormous actor. Brian was yelling, "Hold him! Three, Two, One!"

Taki won the gold. In all of my Judo experience, which amounts to two full days, I've not seen anyone recover from a throw to the floor. But here, with Brian on the sidelines calling out some genius plays, and Taki skillfully interpreting the instructions, he popped out of the danger zone and turned into Spiderman with his elbows out and somehow into a web pressing down on the seemingly lifeless movie star. Afterwards Taki was panting.

To Brian he said, "You bastard! Letting me flip you all the time in practice. It doesn't work in real life!"

Brian replied, "You won!"

Taki said, "I won on the ground. I can see the ground is my future. Six feet in the ground."

NO MATTER

AT THE window of her hotel room overlooking Ocean Drive and the waning afternoon, she daydreamed. At street level in front of the hotel a band plucked out a flamenco. Neighboring hotels competed with music of their own, so that all the sounds merged and rose to the sixth floor, in a hypnotizing stew. But it was the wind that caught her attention, bashing at the blinds, sounding like a gigantic jaw crunching on bones.

Juan was across the street, sitting on a low wall. He was waiting. He would know her when he saw her. Meanwhile she was sliding the room key into her pants pocket, and stopping in front of the hall mirror where she examined herself. "See you later," she murmured, and walked out.

Daylight dwindled to twilight and despite the gale she made for the beach. Toward the regiments of white and blue umbrellas planted at angles, creating walls of flapping canvas with which to protect the tourists from the sun. The lounge chairs were mostly empty.

Long before she slipped out of her red flip-flops and tucked them behind a trash can, Juan shadowed her. She wrapped her cardigan tightly around herself and pressed against the rough wind, and toward the eerily placid surf. When she shivered she blamed the breeze.

In the foam of the surf she let her toes nibble at the water. She was surprised by the warmth of the liquid, which she could scarcely feel. In a trance she stared as the froth rolled over her painted toenails.

"Are you alone?" came a question from a man suddenly beside her. She summed him up as a shade beyond the bloom of youth, with his start of a paunch. Almost handsome with his shiny black hair.

Juan was smiling, broadly, and hoping he was concealing the adrenaline. "May I walk with you?" he proposed. In an instant he had slunk to her side and swiftly they were arm in arm. She did not like the feel.

"My grandmother always took me to the sea," he said, as they strolled. She noticed his white button-down shirt was missing a button at the collar where a thread hung loose. "My grandmother would jab with her rosary and say, That way to Cuba, Juanito, promise me one day you will take the family home," Juan laughed. "I love my grandmother so I always told her, 'Si Abuelita!'"

He hopped around so that he was walking backwards in front of her, grinning confidently. "Shall we take a drink? My apartment is..." And he was indicating a tall building. "There is my apartment. Let's go and take a drink on the balcony, Si?"

Smiling, she shook her head and she took a step away. Whereupon he was on her. From nowhere he grew fangs and claws and he was pulling her to the sandy ground. In a wordless squall they folded into the lapping waves. All matter disintegrating with the elements.

THE DOLLHOUSE

I HAVE tumbled on some good luck. A friend, a local with a thirty year foothold on this glorious island I like to call home, well he tipped me off on the sudden availability of a certain dwelling.

A cottage is how it was described, on a lane I had never heard of. It took a few passes and u-turns to even find the street. And then the little house, like a fallen diamond earring, its luster gummed from the dusty path and its brilliance obscured with tangled overgrowth, the interior dulled from years of encrustations from the previous tenant, an antisocial type, who moved home to live with his mother.

I have relocated a dozen times this past month. Many options flew my way but each was the wrong sized bowl of porridge and again and again I plunged the possessions back into my car and moved my tawdry sideshow along. An unexpected lowlight was the gorgeous roof dwelling, where I had my hammock delivered, and did spend a few nights before discovering I could not stay. For one thing the property was a construction site, and for another it was infested with rats. A highlight was a week at the Sugarloaf Lodge, a few Keys north, where I reveled in a hugely comfortable room frozen in the 1950s. With its view of the mysterious mangrove islands and sunsets and crocodile sized iguanas with scaly crests and fingers like scimitars, I could happily have lived there for the rest of my life. But hotel life gets pricey.

And then my friend wrote me and tipped me off about the cottage. Reluctant to get my hopes up lest they be dashed I went to see it.

And I'll admit I wasn't swept off my feet at first sight. Especially as I could barely find it, lost as it was in the underbrush.

Over the past few days I have conducted an army of skilled artisans and the place is transforming into a doll house. Even the underbrush is on the schedule for clearing and an area of the miniature garden has been allocated for the hammock, which must now be brought over from the rooftop stop. Seeing as, I think, I dangled it as a 'house warming' gift, effectively I will be stealing it.

As the diamond earring polishes up to a stunning gloss I'm liking it all more and more. I think I'm going to be there for a while.

ENCHANTMENT

I MISSED a Thanksgiving party because I couldn't find my clothes. The greatest challenge to sofa-hopping is trying to find one's stuff. Everything of mine is between a storage unit and every square inch of my car. For one reason or another I moved nine times since November 1st.

One extra illegal night at my previous rental, cruising out at five in the morning so as not to be reported on by the neighbors. Then one night at the rooftop house, which didn't work out on account of a giant rat. On to friend Martha, followed by a visit to the Judo pals in Miami. Back to Martha's, then one night at Julia's, then back to the rooftop for one night, immediately retreating to the Palms Hotel. Back to the rooftop, if only in disbelief I was losing ground to a rodent. But he won, and I made my way to the Sugarloaf Lodge after which I ended up back at Martha's, a ridiculously luxurious setting, what with its ninety degree swimming pool, a very hard place to leave.

But leave I did and it is amazing to have reached the end of this journey. Tonight is my first night in the dollhouse. Almost all the paint is on the walls, the rest is on the tile floor, and on my face, spatter patterns telling the forensic tale of my slapdash approach to manual labor. Thank heavens all week long I was accompanied by a slew of talented Manuels, mostly Cubans, all at the ready for artisanal crafting. They made a garden where before there was tundra, and a sparkly clean and usable home where before there was insane asylum ambiance. All was well until the final day of painting, whereupon, disastrously, Manuel the painter was unable to show up, and the chore was left to me. So it is not perfect, and gobs stopped in mid drip, clumping half way down trims, reminiscent of post-eruption Pompeii.

Oh well, it's done, and I'm in. Today I wasted perilous amounts of time admiring the views around my two hundred square foot domain in its fresh shades of greens and blues.

Princess Olga, my maternal grandmother, and I shared a trait in common. We loved miniature things. She had a collection of tiny treasures and we would spend hours at a time handling, ever so carefully, the wee objects and admiring them, marveling at their tininess. There were boxes of gold studded with gems and inside might recline a perfectly made doll with tailored clothes. Or little leather bound books with gold page edges, and the finest delicate German porcelain cups and saucers, far too pretty to ever consider using. Everything entirely useless, coddling a fetish of follies. Closing the loop I am now living in a dollhouse. Miniaturism in vivo. I am enchanted. Even some of the Manuels commented on the tightness of my new quarters. But I know my grandmother would have been enchanted too.

TIME

A FEW days in New York at a pal's. From the second floor window, where puffs of overheated air insisted from the radiators, I watched bundled New Yorkers walking in the cold rain, hands jammed in pockets, hunched tight shoulders, heads cast down, staring at the cement sidewalks they marched across. Quick steps moving them along, they kept to themselves, never making eye contact, everyone isolated in his individual pod of pensées obscure.

From my position I could see directly into the apartment across the street. I watched a man moving around, talking on his phone, withT his free arm performing arabesques. He was smiling widely and occasionally bursting with laughter. I liked the ambiance of him. Then, in a burst, I realized I knew him. I could see the walls of his apartment were smothered with gorgeous paintings. It was artist Ron Ferri and he was gesticulating wildly, chatting on his telephone and obviously laughing. Mountains of time have passed since I've seen this old friend.

Through the years, of all that which I have emotionally bonded with, and then lost, scattering, blown to bits, in the wind, people is all I miss. To call anything 'mine' is to suppose a sense of domination, yet things break, things get stolen, get lost, rot; people die. Ownership is sleight of hand, at best.

It was midday and I was ostensibly on my way to the airport, when I was seized by the urge and I crossed the street and forced my way in. It's an old New Yorker trick to simply push all the call buttons in the foyer, pressing on the little metal nipples, until invariably, contrary to all logic, someone will buzz one in.

The elevator delivered me directly into the spacious apartment and there stood Ron, virtually unscarred by the deluge of time. He was already smiling even though he had yet to recognize me. And then he did, and we both screamed with fun. We hugged hello. Our reunion was rushed, but it was wonderful.

And then I had to run and catch a cab. New York, admittedly, is about as polar opposite as could be found for my hyperborean haven of Key West but I couldn't help wanting to smash in the face of the old couple, reclining in the comfort of their Lexus, and squinting at me with furled bobbed noses, honking their car horn at me because I had deigned to cross the street, in front of them, to flag an oncoming cab. It was raining and I was lugging my luggage for my return flight south. I stopped in front of the Lexus, obliging the car to halt at my feet. The car horn blared away and I smiled the biggest broadest smile imaginable, as I transmitted my feelings of pity for their intolerance, and then, in case they missed my point, I gave them the almighty bird, still beaming at them, making sure to dawdle, and waste some more of their precious time before I languidly stepped away, and caught that cab.

BIRD OF PARADISE

MY FRIEND is waiting on me, he needs my help. I had to tell him I'm so sorry but I'm busy, I'll catch up to him later and lend him a hand, or whatever.

The thing is today I'm dog-sitting, at friend Martha's mansion by the sea where she is the caretaker for some multi-millionaires, and where it is ridiculously comfortable. I got there early with a bag of supplies consisting of Scottish smoked salmon, Belgian chocolates and a flask of dark rum.

Really, my friend is lucky I even heard the phone. If the sun hadn't tucked itself behind a scrim of pale clouds I would still be in the pool, floating on my back with my eyes closed, sopping up the sensation of allowing the cooled pool water to roll over my exposed torso while I'm inhaling the flower flecked air. Paradise.

The pool area at the mansion by the sea, with its wide open views of raucous nature, is closed in with a roof and walls of netting, keeping pesky insects at bay. With Martha's pooch by my side, both of us snacking on the salmon and the chocolates and the rum, I watched a tiny bird slowly freak out. I watched his repeated attempts to find an escape. He knew he was trapped, but he also knew he got in, and therefore, there was reason to keep trying. And yes I feel confident I can paraphrase on his behalf because I observed him and I deduced his intentions, and let me tell you it was heartbreaking. He crashed against the near invisible barrier. Over and over he flew up and smashed his little self against the confusing wall. Bird had tremendous determination and didn't give up. I worried he would break his neck.

Pooch snoozed, uninterested or possibly tipsy, while I opened the two screen doors hoping to lead Bird, demonstrating my purpose by walking through and back a couple of times. Eventually Bird was exhausted and now he rested on the white marble ground, panting slightly, his small shape slumped, his rounded wings hanging despondently at his sides. I was so sad for him, I really felt for him.

Then Bird pulled himself together and once more began hopping along the bottom of the wall of net, he bounced along in short hops, dispiritedly. He looked like a circus actor walking home still in costume, I almost expected him to start puffing on a cigarette.

Instead, this little bird of paradise found the exit, a tear in the net wall just large enough for him to hop through. I missed the moment he crossed the threshold into freedom. But I did see his ecstatic loop-de-loops out over the canal, he was obviously overjoyed and buzzed about in huge circles loudly chirping before flying away, into a black spot on the cerulean sky.

I was flooded with relief at his success. And now I must go help that friend of mine. I could get canonized at this rate.

LIFE WITH PIE

MY PENULTIMATE move before I left town, on my way to New York for Christmas parties, was to drop my bicycle at the bike shop for a tune-up, which would include getting the chain back on the gears. I have been harsh on my green bicycle, plunging off sidewalks and knocking the air out of the tires, all in the name of fun. I knew it was time to take the bugger in when, while riding, a powerful clanking could be heard over my headphones.

The absolute last thing I did before driving myself to Key West International Airport was to stop by Kermit's Key Lime Pie Factory and purchase myself one frozen Key Lime Pie, with my Monroe County resident's discount. The pie, resplendent in its carrying case of bright yellow plastic bag with Kermit's logo emblazoned, caught the attention of local's who called out, "That's the best pie in town!"

Had I known the exponential beneficial effects of traveling with a pie I would always have travelled with one. Usually unsmiling airport staff and security guards and fellow passengers bent over backwards reverentially, you'd think I had the Dalai Lama in a bag. Even the Security Team of screeners broke from their mean glares and offered jokes about how it wouldn't be their fault if only half the pie made it out the other end of the x-ray machines. They were all abuzz and smiling at the very thought of pie.

New York was raucous fun with Christmas parties, each of my four day visit devouring more of me until I was legless and it was a huge relief when I made it home to Key West. Traveling home sans pie was a starkly different experience. I will never leave home without one again.

The first thing I did when I got back was to fetch my bike, oiled and fixed up better than new. Last night I rode around town and everything certainly looked like Christmas. Palm trees and houses and front lawns are decorated with bright blinking lights and inflatable things, with moving parts, candy cane wheels rotating and carrousels set to music and slowly turning spreading their litter of twinkling lights. Cars festooned with Rudolph noses and antlers are double parked outside well-lit houses, while chimneys chuff and scent the mild chill with earthy rich smoke, mingling with the briny sea air, and making it smell like Christmas.

I came home to find the perfect party invites. Friends Christmas Eve, and other friends Christmas Day. And of course I plan on presenting Key Lime pies at every stop. I'm already feeling glutted, and spoiled and I plan on overdoing everything. Especially the fun. I hope the same for everyone.

HAPPY 2013

I WENT to the Jail on Christmas Eve because I felt sorry for the ladies. Meanwhile Sally is right where she wants to be. Inmate #1234 at the Key West Detention Center. "See," she confided to me that evening, "I'm a lesbian." Sally is short, she is wiry and aging abruptly, meanwhile her blue eyes twinkle when she speaks, her head thrown back. "Three hots and a cot, and all the pussy I can eat. If you'll pardon my French, this place is fucking Paradise!"

Later, driving to Sunny's house, I had brought along a Christmas gift which happened also to be contraband, a perfectly rolled joint stuck inside my wallet, and every cop car I passed I considered how I might end up back at the Detention Center. At least I know everyone there.

Sunny read 'Twas the Night Before Christmas, which I'd never heard before. Her boyfriend of near a score years clamped back tears as he watched her. Thirty of us sat in their pretty garden lit with fairy lights laced through the foliage, and under a dark sky with its paths of stars of crushed diamond. It was a beautiful evening.

They mingled their Christmas traditions, his of soup on Christmas Eve, and hers of baking bread, with olives and rosemary. And reading 'Twas the Night Before Christmas".

Drinks were nobody's tradition, 'Drunken Snowmen' which came out of the blender like a white carpet. Into the blender went the contents of many a large bottle, plus a tub of vanilla ice cream and, most impressively of all, whole candy canes, which crunched up to nothingness, at least visibly. I didn't try it.

Next day, on my way to an annual gathering of luminaries I received an invitation from Captain Al and Candace to watch the sunset with them aboard the Reef Chief. I dithered with my options. There was the perfection of the artist hosts, and their friends, and all at the perfect hideaway house down the end of a long driveway, making my decision all the knottier. How to decide? I wanted everything. But I might see dolphins! Gracelessly I dumped the defrosting frozen Key Lime pie, and sped away.

I found them at the wharf, where Captain Al helped me into a white dinghy, and we powered past moored boats and away from the docks. In the harbor we picked up a friendly pirate living aboard his sailboat with two extremely relaxed cats. And then we puttered out to Captain Al's boat, an antique schooner of 65ft, replete with two giant masts and a working canon. Captain Al's home, "I haven't slept on land in twenty years," he announced, smiling into the sun.

Sea life with its twinkling calming ways took over and Time sluiced and churned up deep currents. Toward the end of sunset we saw three dolphins sliding slowly in gentle hoops through the calm cater, dorsal fins slicing against the peach tones of twilight. The dolphins are mesmerizing, like glimpsing Nature winking.

Happy New Year!

NIGHTBIRDS

BLAME IT on the moon but I couldn't sleep. When daylight seeped around the blinds I took a sleeping pill and sunk blissfully asleep. The next thing I knew I woke up to an uncharacteristically grim day. It looked like London outside, the light was pale and thin and strangely gray. So not the tropics, I thought before I realized it was eight at night. Which is probably why, at half past midnight I was restless.

I drove to the Green Parrot, my favorite bar, where a throng milled on the sidewalk outside, always a good sign. I parked at the court house across the street where there is always a space, and into the club I stepped. The bar was very full but I didn't recognize anyone, except for the bouncers and the bartenders to whom I nodded hellos. They know me from sight though none of us have ever spoken. Except for one bartender, an older gentleman with a spiral of gray like a bedspring for a ponytail. After initial hiccups with him trying to make sense of my hybrid accent further distorted by the din, when it became clear I was asking for water I thought I saw a trace of disgust crease his forehead. Ordering a glass of milk might have gone over better. Since this initial skirmish we have developed a system that requires no words. I merely wait, three back in swollen crowds of the well oiled, until invariably he sees me and effortlessly scoops from the depths of a metal cooler with a sliding lid, and as he hands the dripping bottle to me over the heads of the soused I pass him a five dollar bill. It's a great deal for both of us.

The band was an older group with sagging tattoos and gray hair and an impressive aggregate of talent. Four men and a lady and a gold sparkly drum set and all type guitars and an electric piano.

The lady's voice with its soulful clarity stroked your face, making us all fall in love with her. She smiled at her bandmates, galvanizing them as they juggernauted on into the hypnosis of rhythms of their endless original songs, their voices wrapping each others like shimmery linings. Sounds belted out and us dancers moved independently and yet cohesively. Well, except for one amazonian who rammed me and then fell on me, taking us both down to the sticky floor.

When the police came to say the neighbors were complaining and it was long past time to stop we all went mad and demanded "One more!" The cop relented. Only in Key West! It was well after 3am when that last song finished. The bar wasn't closing, it's just the music had to cease. As I sauntered back to my car, imbibing on the nourishing honeysuckle air, I realized I had forgotten about the night crawlers and the mesmerizing mayhem at hand. I'll thank the moon as once more I'm hooked.

ONE MAN'S TREASURE

KEY WEST has many unique features. There are few other places on earth where you can go down to the beach in the morning and reasonably expect to trip across treasure from Spanish galleon shipwrecks.

Equally you could, as I have, sashay into a local pawn shop and you'll be offered slabs of emeralds, supposedly from the Atocha ship. "That's worth sixty-thousand dollars," the pawn shop owner said, fingering a green rock, "But you can have it for thirty grand."

But then I heard a story, and it all began with a man walking into a bar. Key West was settled by pirates and wreckers and naturally, the wet town still attracts those with adventure in their blood. Just like Steve, Tennessee native and contractor by day and treasure hunter the balance of his time.

Time spent mostly under water in the Gulf of Mexico amongst the rotting wrecks and the dolphins and the sharks, with his trusty map in hand. A map he bought off a hungry, nervy character, the man who walked into the bar. This codger had his own reasons, which included a long standing loathing of all things Mel Fisher, and was glad to exchange his hand-drawn map for five hundred bucks today and a promise of more if booty was ever located. After that Steve was on his own, with his map.

And emeralds were located, exactly where the X on the map indicated, in staggering quantities. Almost immediately this find was disputed and discredited by the Mel Fisher conglomerate, everything from the emeralds were fakes to the fact they really all belonged to the Fishers.

Mel Fisher, the man who located the Atocha, has an empire which continues to dominate in the imaginations of believers. Detractors, however, will tell you Mel Fisher has sold twice the treasure he ever discovered. Worse still, allegedly, Mel manufactured some of those antique coins. Another detail Steve will tell you is he has seen the manifesto from the Atocha, a document in the safe keeping of the Smithsonian, and zero emeralds were transported on the Atocha.

Any day now Steve's three year old court case should wrap up, and it is looking favorable to him, which would just about change his life and make him filthy rich. "I'll give it all away," he says, "After I get a new truck. Otherwise, I'm not materialistic at all. But I do love finding things."

It's all about things, Baby! It's all about collecting and hoarding. Speaking of hoarding I got the last of my things out of storage. Each trip I'd peer into other peoples cages and invent stories to go with the objects. One box in particular caught my attention, marked 'Maria's Winter Clothes' and thickly coated with dust. Sweating as I humped my boxes, I was thinking how Maria was spending a fortune storing her winter clothes. I remarked on this when I went to check out. The man behind the desk, interrupted from some guitar playing, said, "Maria is probably dead."

WRITERS ON WRITERS

BETWEEN THE Literary Seminar, a sailing boat race and with the winter influx of snowbirds the tiny city of Key West is currently stuffed to its eyeballs. Even my reliable parking spot behind the courthouse has been discovered, and I'm forced to putter on searching for a free space, like a tourist.

I was lucky enough to have been made a gift of a pass to the Literary Seminar which was a thorough delight. Held in the old Cuban meeting hall on Duval Street the stage was decorated with scrims of Trompe-l'œil bookshelves and every seat in the house was occupied. This was the 31st annual Seminar with a theme of biographers and their subjects. The events were well attended with types come to soak up the bon mots of the participating luminaries, many in the crowd scribbling feverishly into notebooks on their laps.

I made a point of arriving as late as feasible and entering the darkened auditorium and stopping immediately just inside the heavy door. And from here, leaning against the back wall which was oddly padded and thus comfortable, I watched. It was decidedly impressive to listen and absorb the intelligence of these productive and prolific and earnest authors. Yet there was a coliseum feeling of observing terrified victims, even those who managed to appear poised but spoke too quickly or too low, telltale signs of nerves. I was so grateful it was not me up on that stage. Public engagements make me so nervous I miss most of everything. Here I could drink up every last drop.

I listened more than I watched because shaggy heads of hair obscured my line of vision and I could not always see the stage. My attention drifted when the whisperings of a group of women nearby invaded my mind. I shot them an evil look and they gasped and quietened, momentarily.

It kills me to admit this but a lot of the learned utterances were over my head, mentions of writers I've never heard of, let alone read. I felt woefully ignorant and vowed to study a lot more very soon.

My favorite moment was watching Edmund White, a luminary amongst luminaries. He was part of a quartet of writers there to discuss The Quest for the Ecstatic. They sat in high back chairs each with a microphone on a stand before them. The moderator introduced Ed White as the bishop of the proceedings whereupon Ed blessed the audience making everyone laugh. He was clearly not nervous at all and easily held us in sway with his every word. When for a second he couldn't retrieve a thought fast enough he called it Ecstatic Senility, causing a ripple of mirth through the crowd. He wrapped it all up saying Genet was the Proust of the working classes. The applause was ecstatic.

And then the authors shuffled off the stage and the audience stayed motionless, possibly, like myself, they just didn't want for the magical goings-on to end.

MOTOR SKILLS

RECENTLY I made a trip up to the chilly north of West Palm Beach. It was dusk when I began the journey southbound and all around me motorists drove with Kamikaze urgency. Hundreds of steroidal vehicles zoomed all around and I was terrified to even change lanes, and when I did I noticed I was whispering prayers.

After what felt like several anxiety filled hours I was distraught to discover I had yet to pass Miami. Eventually it was late and dark and I pulled off the highway and parked. I sat still for a moment, allowing my body to catch up with the gravitational pull. As the molecules adjusted to time and space I turned on the interior lights and retrieved my stuff, phone, sandwich, etc, as everything had lunged to the floor from so many taps on the brakes. With another hour and a half to get home I rolled around until I was facing the highway where I waited for the oncoming rushing cars to pass and then I dragged out to the road and pressed the gas, spluttering out in a wide arc. Naturally, in the echoingly silent night, I had not used my turn signal.

As I was righting things I noticed, out of the corner of my eye, a parked car. A double take and I spotted the row of lights across the roof. Anxiety stabbed momentarily as, passing, I saw a person within was raising arms to the steering wheel. Cold fear flash-froze me as all the clues fell into place. And then his infernal headlights flamed on, the cruiser appearing to elevate like a hovercraft from hell.

I stomped the accelerator. In my rearview mirror I could see the pulsing progress of the cop. He was coming for me! Adrenaline flooded and I remembered advice from ex-boyfriend Criminal Mike, all those stories he repeated, ad nauseam when he was drunk, all of them starting with, "Back in the day..." and then would unspool some tale of extremely bad choices wrapped up in his endless supply of good luck.

A gentle curve in the road afforded me my chance and I cut the wheel hard and pulled into a parking lot and turned off the engine and the headlights and the interior lights which are programed to switch on for a grace period. A feature designed without the needs of criminals in mind.

With my eyes half closed I stealthily observed Mr Cop cruise slowly by. He was staring ahead and he didn't spot me. I exhaled in a lumpy uneven terror filled manner and talked myself down from the ledge. Criminal Mike had always stressed the importance of patience. He would go so far as to crawl into a hole and sleep for several hours until the coast was clear.

And then Eureka! I watched Mr Cop returning northbound. He had given up his pursuit. I gave it a little longer and then I was free to sail on homeward. Free to gloat at last!

PERSPECTIVE

IMAGINE YOU nodded off in a library and next thing you knew books were skydiving off shelves, instantly metamorphosing into walking talking humans in party attire. Well this was exactly how it felt when recently I attended the joint birthdays of two literary scions at a charming house.

It was a wet dream come true to be among so many of the greatest living artists, all of them at ease and merrily celebrating. No doubt about it, I was awestruck. Allow me to namedrop shamelessly (listed alphabetically, because, really, how else?) while I attempt to recover my composure just thinking of the eminences.

Judy Blume Annie Dillard Alison Lurie Robert Stone Edmund White...and everybody else whose names I've lost track of... I apologize, it was mighty difficult to concentrate while being starstruck to this degree.

Exactly one week later I was parking, involuntarily, outside that lovely house.

According to the three Key West motorcycle cops who detained me, sirens blaring, you do not want to wash your car before you have any kind of accident, because, "It's easier to read what happened if there's dust," one of them said, as he poked at the rills of sticky pollen, bending close to examine. "Like here! If it hasn't been disturbed you know nothing happened."

Turns out some mendacious dumb ass complained I'd scraped the side of her car. And she might have pinned the crime on me except that the marks along the side of her car were black and my car is gray, and furthermore the inch of filth coating my vehicle is perfectly undisturbed and thus absolves me from so much as touching her minivan.

I knew I was innocent but a nervous disposition propelled me into ridiculous small talk about their snazzy boots, knee high shiny black leather jobs with laces at the crook of the ankle, like tiny corsets. I admired fawningly until one officer lamented wryly, 'These boots are awful! Awful hot!"

The cops cracked jokes amongst themselves, the senior officer getting a kick out of torturing the dispatcher by speaking impossibly fast while reciting license plate numbers and incident report numbers so that the dispatcher squawked through the shoulder walkie talkie thingy, and the cops cackled, their belts of dangling equipment jangling like gigantic charm bracelets.

Things always take longer than reasonably necessary when the cops stomp on ones tail. Provided I'm under the sheltering sky of my lilly white world, while things are slow, they do wind up with friendly handshakes and fare-thee-wells.

Parallel realities rubbed shoulders when I spotted superstar Edmund White, in khaki shorts and button down shirt, making his way toward the house, with its overhanging trees and white filigree carved white picket fence. I watched Ed stop and turn and haul himself up the steps to an unlatched door, whereupon he vanished and I snapped back to my reality.

WINNING MOVES

BACHACO, AN established band but new to town entertained last night at the Green Parrot. Sax, trombone, trumpet, couple guitars, the phattest bass player in the world, great drums, oh and those voices, and did I mention His Hotness in the turquoise tee shirt and those bopping hips. Wonderful funk poured from a score of musicians sharing the tiny stage, each jigging in place with instruments pushed to their outer limits.

One of their last tricks was a dance competition, three women and three men leapt to the stage. The men were evidently soused, and possibly didn't know what they were doing, the women, however, got busy flirting unctuously with His Hotness.

A guitarist emceed, starting with the ladies, first a Latina in a filmy low-cut dress with her breasts peeking out like curious dachshund puppies. She had those puppies vibrating. Next went a sultry Caucasian brunette and she swished around to the beat. They were good these girls, they were certainly brave. Last went a Cafe-au-lait lady in a tribal print long dress. She launched with some precise hips, like she was kneading the music. She was making me think maybe I could be up there, even I could do that, I mused smugly. Then, as if she'd flipped a switch she turned her back to us and thrummed her scrumptious rump making the room explode, everyone pulling forward for a clearer look. We were galvanized as one prurient mass, and then she revved up another notch and lowered to the ground, cheeks slicing the air like carving knives, by the time she was motoring back up the entire room was whooping, arms above their heads and applauding. As she buzz-sawed her way to the ground and then pulsed back up, her moves mesmerizing, it was obvious she was winning. I was relieved I hadn't erroneously forced myself on the events. Best for me to watch, and bob discreetly in the crowd.

Next went the men, and it was clear she had inspired them. First a twenty-something, thin and hard like a plank, with stiff pants and a wide belt and a wife-beater and a pork pie hat and he threw himself into a synchronized throb, no doubt he was moving fast, but he reminded me of logs tumbling in a turbulent river. Next were two worrisomely old men of scant hair and much inebriation, and they wobbled dangerously around the tiny stage.

When the emcee declared Mademoiselle Cafe-au-lait the undisputed champion the look on her pretty face was bashful, and she stared down. Her guy, from within the well of dancers, beamed like a beacon, his wide smile and proud eyes glued to her, yet still she looked down. I could see she was smiling and I thought it was as if she knew she had broken a cardinal rule, she had pulled out the heavy artillery at a pocket knife mete. She stepped off the stage and into the open arms of her guy.

THE TRAVELER

ALL HIS life Tommy had diligently followed the rules. Until he turned thirty when he was thunderstruck with wanderlust. Sitting at the kitchen table in the only house he had ever known, sharing cake and coffee with his mother, nervously scraping up invisible crumbs from around his plate, "I need more!" he declared. His mother picked up the knife and made to cut him another slice of cake. "I need a life!" he almost shouted, yanking the knife from her hand. He told her of his plans and she broke down and wept. Tommy promised to write, but he was resolved. Before he left, he sold everything, including his truck.

He kept only a guitar and whatever else he could stuff into a backpack.

Everyone said he had been a cute baby. People fawned over him, occasionally mistaking him for a girl, he had always been slight and what with his shiny pelt of blonde hair and his tiny upturned nose. But he wanted more from life.

He had been 'walking' for the past few months, which in truth involved many a hitched ride. Most often from women. On Christmas Day, somewhere in Texas, a lady in a silver pickup truck stopped beside him on the interstate and kicked open the passenger door, "For heaven's sake!" she yelled at him, "C'mon! Get in! I'm feeding your skinny ass tonight!"

Thanks in part to his still appealing features Tommy was offered space on sofas and guest rooms, but he declined, saying sweetly, "If I may, I'd rather sleep on your back porch. I have a sleeping bag." But he'll make use of the bathroom, and the kitchen, and even another ride to the next oasis. Always maintaining the illusion of roughing it and flexing his imagination Tommy convinced himself he was experiencing freedom.

Sensibly, given the weather, he was headed south. He'd never heard of Key West only a few months before, but now he was walking the last stretch of the road, to the southernmost point in the Continental United States. He walked into paradise and fairly effortlessly found a shelter for the night, illegally nuzzling under the sheltering eaves of an abandoned house near the center of town. Tommy slept under that house for several nights, without incident. It was okay at night, but in the daytime he said, "I do have to come out, with this huge backpack."

Tommy relied on an engaging smile and he easily picked up handyman jobs to keep up a flow of lucre in his pockets. Nightly, he had taken to sitting at the bar of the Green Parrot, with his array of drinks, a beer, a shot, his bag of loose tobacco, he rolled his cigarettes. All his toys giving him the appearance of self-containment, but in reality, they were mere props.

When she entered and ordered a bottle of water he noticed her. After traveling for several months Tommy's instincts were sharpening. "Hello," he said, smiling.

Walking away she noticed twenty bucks had vanished.

THE COLLECTORS

MARC AND Lizzie will tell you they are collectors. Lizzie likes to think she has a better eye than her husband, but "Marc has that dash of rash", she'll tell you, "He's really a genius!"

They were obsessed with things and shopped continually. Saturday mornings they were first at every yard sale. They pet and pampered and fetishized their things. They have a storage unit here in town and when they visit they can't help themselves and they are haggling over the abandoned objects available for purchase at the front desk.

In reality they are hoarders. In reality they have supplanted the value of human beings with things, betting on immortality, perhaps. They are old and possibly they hope shopping and amassing will keep them from dying. After all, how could they die before they have had the time to inventory and archive and display all their precious possessions.

After a few months in Key West, to get to know his new environs, Marc went on some ride-alongs with the police. The cops whetted his expectations by hinting at the lewd scenes they'd be coming across and he was titilated. He also learned about the Baker Act, a Florida institution whereby the insane are divvied up from regular garden-variety miscreants. Marc will tell you he found the ride-alongs, "Fascinating."

Everyone who knew them remarked on how well they got along. "Soul mates", people said, and it appeared Marc and Lizzie had a storybook romance. What nobody saw was how they argued, at home alone in the evenings. Most often the topic was money. A familiar scene was where he was standing over her, screaming at her. "Woman you're spending all my savings! At this rate you're going to leave me in a trailer."

"You're crazy!" cried Lizzie, sipping her wine. "And you're going to make me crazy too!"

Marc hollered, bearing down on her, "You're going to send me to the poorhouse! I'll kill you before I let that happen!" All Lizzie could see of him was his wide open jaw, like a howling wolf, and feel the flecks of his spittle.

Lizzie leapt on Marc and scratched at him. Her nails pealed strips of his skin and blood puckered before leaking into the lines of his face. He would have been able to hold her off if he hadn't been filming her with his cell phone. Still screaming at each other he called the police.

In front of the officers Marc spoke softly and compassionately toward his evidently batty wife. Lizzie, feral with indignation, was unable to contain herself and continued mouthing off. The policemen rolled their eyes in sympathy with long-suffering Marc and they clasped Lizzie's tiny wrists in handcuffs and placed her in the back of a cruiser, off for an overnight at the loony bin.

Marc had no intentions of pressing charges but it was now on record that his filly was one step removed from the nuthouse. And he had it all on film.

LONG ROAD HOME

MARC WAS at home alone perched on the arm of a sofa. He was pawing lustily at a guitar in his lap. He adored this new acquisition, a yard sale find and now his after a successful haggle, possibly the most emotionally charged of all purchases. To Marc this talisman could ward off death, as if God had winked at him, and he grinned as he strummed, liking the sound, liking the peacefulness of single life, if only for the night. He tried to picture his wife's face, but he couldn't get anything, like the fuse box was smashed. He grimaced and felt the hold of the bandaids on his face, pulling at his skin. His wounds began to itch. "Bitch!" he cried, and gently put down the guitar and shuffled off to look at himself in the hall mirror. Marc examined the wounds at close range. Tiny dots of dried blood freckled his face. He began to collect wallet and keys, all he knew was he wanted fresh air.

At the loony bin the smell of bleach and ancient excrement infested the air. Lizzie had noticed a pack of tarot cards on the bookshelf in a waiting room and now she was reading the cards for the nurses, defying the rules of fraternization. Predictably, they were fascinated to hear about themselves and lined up for attention. Lizzie had an odd habit of removing her rings when she read the cards.

On the verge of leaving Marc realized something was off and he flipped back on the lights. His heckles up, instincts shrieking at him from some primitive well. He felt panic, but he stood still, except for the keys in his hand, which he jangled, an aide-memoir. There was a gap on one wall. A painting was missing. Thoughts hurled at him like pelting asteroids and he might have sorted through them more efficiently but his horror was all consuming.

The empty space faced him like a knife thrower, thwack, thwack, thwack as the dreadful possibilities rushed at him, pinning him in place. Where was his treasured painting! Suddenly he rushed from one end of every room to the other, skidding on the soft tiles, he pawed through stacks, he dug into the back of cluttered closets, he swung open doors and landing on his knees ransacked his way through cascades of things. Marc blamed the housekeeper, he blamed the neighbors, he blamed Lizzie.

As Lizzie knew they would, soon the lulled nurses began admiring her rings and nimbly she seduced them, "This sapphire is from a flea market outside Paris. I love Paris," she said as she coddled the tiny object.

Sweat rolling down his face, terror ripping through him he could barely grasp the facts when he found the painting, innocently propped behind the front door. Right where he had placed it the day before. He had forgotten. He had to laugh!

Meanwhile, Lizzie had convinced the nurses to release her, and slowly and determinedly she walked the three miles back to the house.

THE KING OF KEY WEST

DAVID WOLKOWSKY, developer par excellence, is a true Key West treasure and easily the most interesting man in town. I met him a year ago, and I instantly recognized him for the mystical magical man that he is. Thanks to my own eclectic childhood, meeting everyone from royals to reg'lar folks, I know cool, and this guy is the real thing.

An invitation from David is a major highlight and might lead one to any of his splendid palaces about town; all filled with magnificent artwork and orchids in fat bunches fixed half way up a doric column brought back from the east, and everywhere there are photographs of himself with famous friends. And then there is his private island, Ballast Key, a few miles off the southernmost coast. In the interest of full disclosure, yes, I was invited out to Ballast Key, and I did discreetly plant a Serbian flag in the sugar white sand. The island getaway is a confection of airy beach house with unstoppable views and paths leading to sculptures for guests to stumble upon like a trail of candy. Yum.

When I met David Wolkowsky I was delightfully fascinated. He is chic and gentle with a nimble and witty mind, and I along with everyone who has ever met him, adore him. So when, recently, he phoned and proposed I write about his long-deceased friend author Patricia Highsmith I said yes absolutely, gladly. I was thrilled for the opportunity to give back after basking in so much of his hospitality.

I plunged into the assignment and while I noted the wording of the poem is undeniably gorgeous the overall effect made me want to slit my wrists. According to Wikipedia Highsmith was prolific yet beset with the demon depression and no one had a nice word to say about her. While she was respected for her writing skills, her best known being The Talented Mr. Ripley quote after quote described her as "relentlessly ugly". This was dispiriting but I was determined to fulfill this special request.

I phoned David, "Couple of questions," I said, "First off, did Patricia write this about you?" Mercifully he said, "No! I have no idea why she picked that to send me. But she signed it so I had it framed." About Highsmith he said, "I met Patricia in New York. I knew her fairly well and she was always very good company." I was on the verge of revealing my miserable research thus far when I saw the light at the end of the tunnel and I slid in questions about his far more interesting self, garnering nuggets such as his memories, as a young child, of the excitement of riding the Flagler Railroad from Miami to the Keys. David Wolkowsky's childhood was spent, "floating around between Key West and Miami". The Wolkowsky family, having first moved to Key West in the late 1880s, owned properties in "old town" and in 1962 David decided to settle. By 1963 he was managing a brilliant deal to develop a waterfront property near Mallory Square. He is perhaps best known for building the Pier House Hotel, a resort where both Jimmy Buffett and Bob Marley started their careers in the hotel's "Chart Room Bar". Buffett credits Wolkowsky as the first to hire him.

For over half a century Wolkowsky has invested in what is often described as a drinking town with a fishing habit. With environmental and cultural sensitivity David Wolkowsky has saved, restored and built, bought and sold much of the local real estate. He is much loved for helping to preserve the look and feel of this unique port of call. He is a philanthropist quietly and steadily supporting the humanities on many levels. Everything from funding prizes for teachers to helping the homeless to investing in his artist friends. One of his favorite authors is P.G.

Wodehouse, "But," he says, "The only problem is the expectation of a 'Jeeves' which is never be found in real life."

Locals vividly recount every cherished sighting, and they say that when they drive their boats past his island, they gasp and sigh at the perfectness of it all. But I watch tourists soaking up all the loveliness and I have to wonder if they know anything about my friend David, the man who intimately helped create this place they so enjoy. I think I need to push for an official David Wolkowsky Day.

ISLAND LIFE

SPEAKING OF private islands reminds me of a time long ago when I sold up and relocated to a private island in French Polynesia.

My senior year was at a high school in the Rocky Mountains where I met Taha, a Tahitian lass. We bonded over our love of adventure and even engaged in a few explorations of our own devising. After high school Taha went west and I east and for the next decade or so we kept in touch by phone. The years piled up and we toiled in drab jobs. One day Taha learned she had inherited a cute little atoll in Tahiti. In a trice Taha took up residence and invited me to join, "Just bring a bicycle, stay as long as you like," she said. I was tantalized and soon I was extricating myself from a job and an apartment I did not love.

A cab dropped me at JFK and left me in a pile on the curb with my brand new bicycle, my bags and my ticket to ride, and thus began the thrills. First one plane to LA and then another out into the middle of the Pacific Ocean. We landed in Papeete in a hurricane and were advised by the police to immediately seek shelter. My bike had been crushed by so many handlers so I dragged the thing out of the airport and there was Taha. We hugged and shrieked, as females do, and then we drove for half an hour past trees bending horizontally and metal roofs peeling from houses. At last we parked in a gated garden bordering a bay. Half a mile out was the island, a bushy green headdress of palm trees. "We'll come get your stuff tomorrow," said my hostess, locking up the car. We hopped into a canoe and Taha paddled us off to paradise.

That night we got plastered and Taha played the ukelele quite at odds with the noisy storm. Next morning Taha handed me a cup of coffee and then startlingly, she dashed up a palm tree and untwisted a coconut which she slashed with a machete and poured the milk elixir into our coffees. I was stunned. "I'm never leaving!" I declared and we clanked cups. We got back in the canoe and oared across to the mainland to fetch my stuff. Scattered on the sandy ground all around the car were glass particles, like snow. The back window was smashed. And all my gear was gone, including the bike.

Later, back on the island I met Taha's boyfriend. Turned out he would be living with us and this might have been tolerable except they were forever squabbling, their screaming and yelling thoroughly dismantled my communing with nature. I began to wonder what exactly I was doing here, swatting at mosquitos, scratching at bleeding ankles and I began to miss the sounds of squealing traffic and sirens and the smell of soot.

It wasn't long before I bought a ticket out, and I was gone. A full scale retreat.

SWINE FLU

SPLAYED ON the sofa in the living room, he watched her. She was boiling water in the kitchen. He hated her. The sight of her, the smell of her, the sound of her voice. He had no idea when this had started, when things had disintegrated.

"Sniff!" he snorted, crumpled tissues all around him, one soggy tissue still grasped in his tight grip. And that's when he felt the creep of a sneeze, like crazy tentacles switching at the back of his throat, stirring up the impulse for a sneeze, gathering speed, like bellows filling the back of his brain, the top of his esophagus and then he was a canon of spume, particles loosened free and he worried all of him would eviscerate and funnel out through nostrils flaring like stampeding horses. "Aaarrrr," he lamented, so sorry for himself, "Oh good Lord!"

He could see his wife at the stove, her elbow raising and dipping and reconfiguring the folds of her frumpy cardigan. He hated that cardigan, he was sure he had told her. Yes, he remembered clearly telling her as much at the Christmas party last year. Maybe she had forgotten, after all, it was a year ago. An entire year! He was shocked and he tried to sit up, with his arms waggling he grappled through the air, shunting himself to the lip of the sofa, but momentum let him down and he petered out, curled over rounded back right over his pajama clad legs, and coughing like a back-firing car, he hacked and hawked. "Aaarrrr!" he exhaled and, still coughing, collapsed into the welcoming embrace of blankets and cushions. He lay still, and stared at the ceiling, one arm dramatically outstretched to the crumb specked floor with the other draped across his face.

Through half closed eyes he peered at her and her wide back and that awful sweater. He had told her it looked like she had put on a few pounds but it didn't seem like she was doing much about it. He hated his life and it was all her fault. All his friends agreed. She had been a big mistake. "Aaaaarrrr!" he wailed, and though he missed it, his wife turned to look at her pitiful partner, she felt for his suffering.

As she turned to him, with his cup of chamomile she breathed in deeply on the scalding damp rising from the tea, like it was a spaceship to escape in. As she placed the mug beside him on a low table she hoped she was not going to catch whatever horrible ailment he had.

"There, my darling," she murmured.

He clawed for the cup and then he whacked at it, boiling water airborne. "You always fill it too full!" he shrieked. "I want a divorce!"

Discreetly she smiled as she watched the hot water roll into the crumbs that speckled the floor, engorging them to tiny islands.

SEMANA SANTA

SPEAKING OF adventure, there was a time long ago when I worked for a literary agency. My job was to read and reduce the unsolicited manuscripts. It was midwinter and I was occupying someone's empty beach house in the Hamptons.

Every Monday I would ride a dirty train into the city, impossible to even see out of the scratched up green hued windows, casting the world in oxidized metal. I would board at a wood carved train station half hidden by pillows of snow out at the end of Long Island, and a few hours later arrive in the sooty dank tunnels that eventually pop one out into the very heart of the city. Shocked into the noise and bustle I'd jostle my way the few blocks to the agency, a tall grey building in amongst innumerable tall grey buildings. Sign in, nod to the attendant and wait in a damp huddle for an elevator.

At the agency I would deliver my reports and cram my backpack with as many fresh manuscripts as I could carry. Back home I'd crank the heat which came through the carpeted floor, I'd brew endless cups of tea and lying on my back, head propped on cushions, I'd spend the week reading my way through the stack.

Largely, the manuscripts were mind-numbing dreck. A disproportionate quantity were submitted by housewives from Seattle, I surmised with too much time on their hands due to the excessive rainfall keeping them all indoors and wistful. My reports invariably nixed their hopes. Until one day, along came a manuscript describing the journey of a group who traveled from California in their own Cessna, sometime in the 1970s, with the goal of visiting the Galapagos Islands. Each chapter saw them further south, leap frogging obstacles and filling with excitement.

I turned the pages swiftly, gripped, I wanted so much to be with them. At the end of reading I wrote my report. For the first time I could recommend a work for publication. l added an addendum, it went something like: PS: I liked this M/S so much I am compelled to leave immediately and travel. Please accept this as my letter of resignation.

I bought a ticket to Belize, a country where I knew no one and knew nothing of my environs, and immediately I felt like I could breathe. I made my way to Ambergris Cay where I took a cheap room above a liquor store. The view of my immediate future was inspiring.

Keeping to myself I took busses south and then west into Guatemala, scaled ancient ruins, photographed gigantic birds floating up high. Then more long bus rides into northern Honduras where I crawled about over more ruins and then more bus rides the length of the Caribbean country, onward I traveled south, ever further south, Nicaragua, Costa Rica and Panama whence I was obliged to fly to Ecuador. Two months had passed and I was in the back of a pickup truck sharing a ride from Quito to Guayaquil, the port town from where one caught the boat to the Galapagos Islands.

I was so close to my goal and so exhilarated by my journey I didn't notice the implications of the start of Semana Santa, their Easter festivities. It was quite a surprise to find not only the town was closed up shut, the entire country was on holiday. Alone in my hotel room I realized I was out of money and had no access to funds.

So, I never did get to the Galapagos, but I did clear my stifled mind with an excellent adventure.

YARD SALE

THAT SAME night as Lizzie walked home, Marc decided his nerves were frayed so he put away his guitar, helped himself to a whiskey and got into bed. No sooner had he slid off to sleep when he was awoken by a splattering crescendo. Bleary eyed Marc got up, pulled on his robe (Burberry, from a yard sale) and went off to explore the reason for the ruckus. He unlocked a door and stepped out into the courtyard and the jasmine scented air. Wearily Marc scanned his territory, tightening the belt on his robe. Even the shadows were layered with shadows, even the sliver of moon only momentarily flashed in between dark fronds of palms. Marc's eyes picked up nothing.

Marc stared into the darkness and he was about to turn around and go back indoors when a noise came from the ground.

"Darling!" he heard and he jumped on the spot and then he looked down to see his wife Lizzie laying on her side, like a baby seal.

"Darling," she whispered again, "I climbed the wall!"

"What? Are you ok?" Marc bent down beside her, thoughts racing incoherently as he helped her to her feet, the both of them wobbling dangerously, the weight of each other almost too much to bear.

"How do I look?" Lizzie asked, smiling wildly.

"Darling, you look wonderful!" he said, but she looked awful is what he thought, a welt developing on her forehead.

"You know today is Saturday!" Lizzie continued. "We have to go to the yard sales!"

Meanwhile, minding my own business at the crest of the new day, I was just getting ready to leave the Green Parrot, my favorite bar. I didn't want to go home but the bouncers were fitting bolts across the closed up boards that serve as windows, when copies of The Citizen, the local daily, flapped in through the still open door. I grabbed a copy, paid up, and muttered my goodbyes. I drove through an unfurling town, with the sky morphing from midnight blues to aquas, down dewy streets thick with greenery and the prettiest of gingerbread houses when I saw a hubbub up ahead.

I was half way down Southard Street, headed north and home, when I was blocked by a couple tussling in the narrow street. In front of one of the prettiest of old houses, grey and white clapboard and shaped like an octagon and all surrounded by two floors of porches, like a dowager in her pearls. On the short sloping lawn out front were tables piled-high with higgledy-piggledy whatever. But blocking my route was a tall man with a scruff of orange hair and tiny bandaids on his craggy face and he was fighting with a thin lady with a huge bruise on her forehead. They had some object in their hands, they were screaming at each other, pulling on the thing between them.

I pulled over, skidding in sand, and parked in a puff of dust.

DREAMS OF GOLD

I AM exclusively selling my new book on my website for Byzantine reasons to do with anti piracy efforts none of which I expect will work very well. I expect the ramparts to give way after a simple battering. Yet my warrior blood impels me to at least try to hold some ground. This translates into me and a box of fresh pressed books, dedicating each in thick felt tip, wrapping and sealing them in puffy envelopes, and hauling the lot to the post office.

I was a couple of humans from the front of the line when I engaged in conversation with a native American, or so he claimed, a man who appeared neither noble, nor wise, nor spiritual, not even a supreme horseman. Arguably his blood has authentic Caloosa DNA and the spit-up of malaria carrying mosquitos. But his concerns were confoundingly plebeian. The Caloosa, with his odd habit of tilting his bald head back and closing his eyes, would expound on his previous commute from a stay in Mastic Shirley, Long Island to an office at the center of Manhattan, "Two and half hours in each direction!" he repeated, and shook his sweaty bald head, eyes closed.

"Next" the attendant called and off shuffled Caloosa.

One more person in front of me, 'Walter the good pirate' is how he introduced himself and he certainly looked the part, with earrings and hair swept into a ponytail, knee length overcoat and a tricorn hat with a yellow budgie clinging disinterestedly at the brim.

By day these pirates and treasure hunters are fishing guides and contractors and the float of drywall coated him, even his teeth. Mouthwateringly he told me he had access to a treasure map, had even made preliminary dives to inspect the trove and sure enough it's the real thing. Walter showed me cracked photographs of grayish lumps and barnacle clad clumps, "Those are gold coins and emeralds!" Walter was whispering, holding the pictures low and close.

I was so impressed, shoving my specs onto my face. "When will you go fetch all this?" I was drooling a bit. "Can I have some?" I asked, whining, forgetting my manners, entranced by the possibilities, imagining tiaras and full matching sets of cleavage-crushing heavy jewels. The way jewels were meant to be.

"Never," Walter said fiercely. "As long as I'm alive, and now my son Little Wally is getting interested, we will be stewards and protect this important history. That's how I see the world," he continued, sliding his photos back in an oily pocket.

"Next!" called the attendant.

Finally I was at the front of the queue when a short official bustled from within and declared, "The building is being evacuated. This is not a hoax. ...white powder was found in an envelope... We're taking precautions. We're evacuating now!"

So out I went into the white blinding sun, kicking my way through the roosters and hefting my box of first to be shipped honest to God sold books, temporarily thwarted.

PARTY TIME

I JUST read Levels of Life; by Julian Barnes, his latest, and I'm a fan, of sorts. However, long ago, Julian Barnes wrote a book called Staring at the Sun, about a woman and her ordinary life sliced up in cartoonishly large leaps of twenty year intervals. At the time I remember thinking it implausible, these spans leaping ahead in twenty year lumps. For a leap, that seemed improbably enormous. Ah, the myopia of youth! All these years later I clearly see the possibility of vast chunks of time sucked away into a blurry tear in Time's fabric.

And now here I am, so much older and I look back on my life, and I see when the trajectory for adventure truly began. Right before my 30s I entirely gave up on anything conventional, and I have been 'on the road', so to speak, ever since. My first divorce was so long ago I don't remember much about that marriage, like the dude's name, but what I do remember is that after seven years of marriage there came a time of critical mass. It was stay and breed and do the wife thing, or bail and toodle off to parts unknown. I took the latter course, I packed up the husband and sent him off to Italy. "I'm right behind you," I lied when I kicked him out of the Toyota truck at JFK. And that was the last time I saw him.

Tomorrow I'm headed for New York City, for my party, to celebrate my new book. I have invited all and sundry from all stages of my life, finally mixing everyone altogether, like the end of a great day of work for a painter with his pallet smeared with bright oils.

Today I examine my choices, and my expectations, and with the benefit of so much time passing, I can critically assess. Most notably I will say it has gone fast. Cresting the precipice of middle age was not even noticeable. There was no peak of Everest moment, no instant where I stuck a flag into a mountain top and felt my goals in my grasp. Far from it. Rather, I feel I am in a holding pattern, a sort of long stalling idle, where all my goals are still just ahead, just around the next mythic corner.

I'm looking forward to seeing my old friends, a little concerned to reveal my aged self. Will any of us recognize one another?

I wish Julian Barnes the best with his new book and thank him for his provocative insights. Turns out he was absolutely right about time hurtling, and now I try and savor the moment, try and appreciate the gorgeous smearing bright oils that comprise my life.

Speaking of books, and friends old and new, I wish anyone who can, please come and say hello at my party Wednesday, 24th April, 6-8pm, at the Vanessa Noel Boutique 158 East 64th Street, NYC.

STUDIO 54

WHEN I was nineteen years old I was stunned to find myself back in New York. The only thing I was sure of was I did not want to live and work in this city, my birthplace. I had tried one year of that and it hadn't appealed. Now I was back from backpacking around the world, on my own, for the previous six months. The idea was I would travel the earth and thereby discover my purpose, my calling. Nothing of the sort happened. I did experience an eye-popping quantity of stimuli but six months later I was back where I had begun, New York City.

And then, by some sort of divine intervention I met Carmen D'Alessio, an energetic Peruvian sexpot public relations queen. Carmen is best known for being the spark plug behind the components of Studio 54.

When I first met Carmen, pretty much on the spot she offered me a job as her assistant. On a lark, and without any visible alternatives, I took the post. Days were all about phoning her hundreds of contacts and inviting them to her parties, at Studio 54, it was an easy sell. Thus I learned everyone's name, inadvertently even learning their telephone numbers by heart. Nights were all about escorting Carmen, in stretch limousines, along with her forever rotating entourage of hot young men. They truly adored her, and she ruled with a powerful bass laugh and thunderous commands, she was a worshipped general.

We motored around the city, stopping in at every happening club, doormen opening ropes and ushering our posse in with personal greetings to Carmen, like she owned the city, and there we would hand out tickets to Studio 54, to anyone who caught Carmen's fancy. We would work our way from club to club, seining effectively for the cutest catch. Eventually ending up at the great club Studio 54 itself.

If anyone displeased Carmen she would have them tossed out of the club. But if she liked them she might take them home with her. My most important role was to arrive at her apartment at eleven in the morning and put on the kettle. Next I would wait for the man, and there was always a man, who would emerge, bleary, staggering, from her bedroom. It was my responsibility to debrief him of his name, as invariably he was a 'freshie', Carmen was not one keen to snack on leftovers, (unless she married, which she did often, but that's another story). So I would ask their name and then show them the front door. By then the kettle would be boiling and I would make a cup of herbal tea and bring it into the still dark bedroom. And give it to my boss, along with the name of her previous night's conquest. And she'd thank me and explode with that wonderful rich laughter, and our day would begin again.

While not necessarily the meaning of life, that was one of my favorite jobs.

BAD CRAB

THE WAY I heard the story there is an inland river, up the Keys a ways, and in the river lived a large blue crab. This crab kept to itself, not only because it was a crab, but because it was always grumpy and whining and complaining. Even amongst other crabs this crab was bad.

But one day this bad crab was obliged to engage with the rest of the crab population. There was a referendum, or something political, and all crustaceans had been called together to vote on a issue of the riverbed and how it was being despoiled. Something to do with those dastardly humans and their need to ruin things with bridges and footpaths and, worst of all, roads.

The bigwig crabs at the meeting were busy shouting at each other and pontificating, and not much of anything was getting done, beyond venting.

Meanwhile, at the meeting, this bad crab was crouched, sort of minding his own business from the periphery of the group when a lady crab he liked scuttled close by. She was beautiful this lady crab, she had tattooed her shell with patterns like filigreed silver. She was very theatrical, for a crabette, and despite himself he couldn't help his feelings. He thought perhaps he loved her, but he hated her too. Because one time, not that long ago, he had sidled up to her, and let his feelings be known, and she had laughed at him.

Now here he was, close to her and she appeared to be alone, and to have acknowledged him. Could it be, he pondered, that she had changed her mind about him. Women! he thought, Well I'll certainly give it another go. So he scurried over to her, and close she was all the more beautiful, and he told her so. "You are beautiful Ms Crabette," he said.

For her part, she just watched him with middling interest. She thought maybe she knew him, but she couldn't be sure. He was a specimen to stare at.

It was more than awkward and then finally she spoke. "Do I know you?" she asked, and then she waited.

The bad crab was shocked into silence, he was frozen quiet, and his tiny mind went blank. How could she not know him, it didn't seem feasible.

Suddenly, a large shiny green crab appeared, crashing through the crowds of crustaceans. He was wider and shinier than the others and he came and stopped beside the girl, slipping his claw through hers, sliding it around her waist, pulling her close to him.

The bad crab had trouble recovering his composure. This was everything he had not expected. Now that he thought about it he didn't know what he had expected.

"I was going to tell you that you have some dirty marsh grass stuck on the back of your shell, that's all I was going to tell you!" the bad crab declared, waving his long claw as he spoke, and then he dragged himself away, muttering and grumbling.

SATURDAY NIGHT IS ALRIGHT

THE JAIL writing class is voluntary and no special dispensation is offered anyone beyond the gratification of a couple of distracting hours. Those who attend, about twenty, are made up of an evolving array of faces. Some are still there since before my first visit last summer, others pop in for a quick stint, never to be seen again. And then the third group, those who come and go and know the rules better than the guards, know the laws better than their court appointed lawyers. Yet, for myriad reasons, they return.

At 7:30pm on Saturdays, Candace (my fearless leader and program creator of twenty years) and I hand in our IDs at the main check in area, and after a brisk frisk of our persons and possessions we make our way. Buzzed through thick doors, and along corridors painted the color of untanned Caucasian skin, deep into the interior of the structure, to the ladies wing.

Here we enter a classroom and gradually the ladies roll in. Once everyone is settled, to warm things up we assign a five minute writing exercise. For example, one week we asked them to write their bio, for a book jacket. Or we'll create a scenario, e.g.: you have just woken up, it is morning and you are in a desert, beside you is a cat and a red pillow. What happened? Last night we brought in fake mustaches for us all to wear during class, and then asked them to write about what it might be like to go on a date with a werewolf. We had some laughs!

At the end of class we give assignments for them to write through the week, to read at the following week's class. Candace and I then add their work to a website we've made www.writeonpublished.wordpress.com. When we return with comments from the general public, the satisfaction they experience is palpable.

Depending on their strengths we might assign custom themes. For example, one lady, a grandmother, is writing an expose of the jail system as seen and experienced through her eyes. She signs off as Anon, as she is already in enough trouble. Her writing ably covers needlessly brutal shake-downs and ritual bureaucratic messes.

Another lady, a mother of two, is writing a children's book. She is off at real prison now, finishing up her sentence but promises she is writing and sending the filled notebooks to her mother for safekeeping. As soon as she is out we will see about getting her work published.

Puke, a girl really, in her early twenties, with a brilliant mind and a love of adventure writes such funny poems she has developed a fan base. Puke ran away from home at twelve years old to ride the trains. Today she sits in jail for a minor infraction, filling her time by reading and writing and dreaming of freedom.

Saturday nights used to be the longest night, one lady said, now it's something to look forward to. Ditto, I say.

NIGHT LIGHT

FOR REASONS beyond my control I was raised in the rain prone United Kingdom, so I am partial to the rain. I love the rain even more so here in the tropics, when the sun is lost in watery clouds and all recognizable sounds of life are replaced by the clattering downpour, meanwhile the air is sweetly spiced and warm.

I was at home, lolling in my white armchair, watching the hypnotic storm outside my windows and I was lulled asleep. I know I fell asleep because I recognized my dream, more a recurring nightmare that I have traipsed through for decades where I am in a vaguely familiar house, it is dusk and the place is consumed by shadows. I am afraid of the dark, especially in this dream, and I rush from room to room flipping the switches on the walls, trying the lamps, but no lights illumine. Occasionally a lamp will light momentarily, like a sneer, before turning off, leaving me in a darker darkness, and filling with anxiety and scurrying in the encroaching night.

Waking me with a thrum was Martha sending a text, asking if I would like to housesit the mansion by the sea for a few days. Yes, I replied. The mansion is two miles from my home, but I had no intentions of leaving once I got in. I cancelled my plans for the week, stopped in at the grocery store for provisions, and drove over.

It was late in the afternoon when I arrived and the storm continued unabated so I was rushing from my car to the front door with my kit and I never noticed the blue and red crabs concealed beneath the lips of the flagstone steps, burrowed into their caverns, just the tips of their front claws hinting at the edge.

Still dripping, I kicked off my boots and made for the kitchen. I lit a stick of incense and made a cup of tea and then I went to select a bedroom, there being so many. With tea in hand, and sliding in my socks, I followed the corridors towards the bedrooms. I never saw the spider on his cobweb but I felt the sticky threads as they applied themselves to my forehead. One hand instinctively patting my face, my hair, and then I found him. A wriggling ball of momentum, his flickering legs pricking my fingertips, and all of him caught in the fibrous net. I screamed. I dropped my cup of tea, scalding myself as I ripped at the insect scrabbling for his life. Dislodged in a tuft of hair I threw him to the ground.

It was early evening by now, and the bedroom was cast in gloom. I flicked the light switch by the door, but nothing happened. So I leaned down and squeezed the switch of the bedside lamp and the light turned on, washing the blue and white room in a friendly glow. But only for a second. Then it flickered off.

SATURDAY NIGHT

STORM SEASON gathers with steamy days of solid rain, interspersed with earsplitting lightning jags. The dusty ground is churned to swamp. The intrepid paddle their kayaks down Duval Street. So much rain fell that mushrooms, like bronzing melting marshmallows swollen in the bases of the potted plants in the garden, have emerged. And butterflies dark and large as vampire bats cling to the windows. Between their furry wings I watched the neighbor's cooler floating down his driveway.

Finally there was a spate of dry long enough for the streets to drain and the sidewalks to pucker dry. I drove downtown and parked near Mallory Square. The first action I encountered was a swarm of cop cars, lights slashing about, nosed in and surrounding a dustup at the crossroads of Greene and Duval where a chauffeur driven stretch limousine was headfirst plowed into a red plastic electric golf cart type thing.

Sloppy Joe's was happening, and the band was very convincing, but then they announced they needed to take a short break. So off I went, merging with the street.

The Lazy Gecko often works for me with good bands, but not so much tonight, where it was simple stuff for the very drunk to sing along to, songs with refrains like "Git me more beer!"

I sauntered down the great main artery that is Duval Street and observed the Homo Sapiens at play and made my mental jottings as I went. Sometimes stopping entirely and leaning against a wall to better catch the sights and sounds.

Before too long I had wandered up the few steps to Willie T's and sat at the bar while the band of three meandered through a handful of songs. Unfortunately, they appeared committed to a sing-a-long with the audience, the lead guitarist going so far as to conduct the helpless sots with a stiff finger, to cue them, as they tumbled against each other and teared up as they belted out the few lyrics they could recall. It was funny until it was pitiful and I pushed off, heading down narrow Appelrouth Lane, pausing in the doorway of Virgilio's, the tiny club with a tree growing in the middle of it. A tree out of which, allegedly, snakes tumble. I peeked in and caught a taste of a band of original hippies, so stoned they lounged on their amps.

Last stop, The Green Parrot. The irony of the Green Parrot is that not permitted entry to its hallowed sticky halls are green parrots, or parrots of any stripe for that matter. But that is not an issue for me as I travel solo. I love the Green Parrot, it is my trusty friend of a bar and upon approach some jamming tunes emanated and sure enough I saw excellent bassist Matt Shuler from Miami up there on the stage with two others, and the sounds were funky and wonderful, and I have to wonder what took me so long to get back there. It's been a while.

A STRONG HAND

THE TROUBLE was I windsurfed to Saudi Arabia. The one time I attempted this sport I grasped the standing part, and I could do a decent job of staying up and traveling in any direction the wind would take me, but despite a week of lessons I could not learn how to turn the thing around. This was 1986 and I was in Jordan at the time, a guest of the late King Hussein and his fourth wife, the cool tall blonde half American half Syrian Queen Noor.

When I windsurfed to Saudi Arabia I was rescued by a flotilla of the King of Jordan's servants who motored out and gathered me up and into their boat and lashed my sailing device off the stern, back to the Palace on the Gulf of Aqaba.

One day the King took me, and some other guests, in his power boat. He said it was the big brother to a cigarette. It sure went fast. All of us with crazy hair zagging to the side as we clung to padded handles and smiled at each other and felt the chattering of teeth from the force.

Then we slowed and bobbed nearby a promontory of crags with some sort of structure atop it. "Now we are in Egypt," The King told us, and then he revved the power boat and we zoomed away, back to Jordan, keeping wide of Israeli waters and an eye out for submarines.

Also visiting were the King and Queen of Spain, Juan Carlos and Sophie. Cousins of mine whom I knew since childhood.

There were times we joked we had a strong poker hand, with two Kings, two Queens and a prime minister. A highlight was one day, over lunch, witness to an extraordinary conversation between the King of Jordan and the King of Spain as they good-naturedly and a touch competitively compared notes on the multiple assassination attempts made on their lives.

This was the occasion of my first wedding, to a Brit whose mother was friendly with the late King Hussein. It was a marriage arranged speedily. After a brief courtship the future hubby and I boarded a flight to Jordan, with a wedding cake from Harrods, and my future ex-husband's mother. I invited no guests, looking for a fresh clean slate, but the groom's mother was our witness at the wedding ceremony, held in the half excavated half restored tomb of Moses, on a hill overlooking the Dead Sea. Before the King flew us away in his helicopter we set free white doves.

Setting the tone for this marriage my mother-in-law remained with us on our honeymoon. Seven years later I would return hubby to his mother. All yours, I thought, and moved on with my life and gradually forgot about the details of this episode. Until today when I started opening up boxes and looking at old photos, having a laugh at the ancient memories and wondering if it's time to try windsurfing again.

VOICE OF OX

DYSLEXIA AFFLICTS a quarter of humanity. I am a member of that quarter and I am at the mercy of the misfiring synapses. Spelling, therefore, is a nightmare for me. School was pockmarked with fraught experiences with exasperated teachers. I was frequently written off as a moron (that, of course, is another story).

Unhelpfully, my first couple of decades on earth I was ferried to and from the USA and the UK. And so began a lifelong tango twixt the myriad distinctions of American English and English English, where sometimes words are spelled the same but pronounced differently and vice versa. I was deeply confused. I muddled on and learned a few rules but otherwise I have relied heavily on the gamut from moldy old dictionaries to the current luxury of electronic spell check.

When in school, all fourteen of them, some in America and some in England, I felt like saying, look grownups, I'll learn your crazy system if you can just simplify things. Instead it was the opposite, with opposing sides of the Atlantic clamoring theirs is the true spelling or pronunciation.

Since school and the need for 'perfection' I have found dyslexia to be a boon. The swarm of possibilities in my mind's eye throws up a plethora of options. For my style of writing this is useful. As to the spelling, well I rely very heavily on spell check. Though not entirely. Sometimes it says, 'No Guesses'. I find this a bit rude. At any rate, at that point I resort to the mighty net where I will certainly find my word. In some instances, however, I don't know that I am wrong. For example, 'peek' and 'peak'. Turns out I've been using the wrong one for years- and I only just sorted this out.

I do apologize to those of you who not only know how to spell but are offended by my mistakes, like my friend George who pounces avidly on every error. Please forgive me. It is not done to annoy.

Recently I have toyed with learning Serbian. Some preliminary investigations have led me to a daunting discovery. The Serbs use two alphabets, one of which is similar to our Roman letters but different, graffitied with slashes on the steeples of certain letters and peculiar victory signs atop others. Then there is Cyrillic, and if old Cyril had intended to compete with the Navajos to make a most uncrackable code of a language, he succeeded. Serbian is a beautiful sounding language, but intimidating to master. For one thing I'm still having trouble with the intricacies of my native tongue.

Anyway, again, apologies for the mangling. Perhaps it's time to deliver the goods in a new format. Perhaps audio is the way to go. Then you'll just have to deal with the nuttiness of my mid-Atlantic accent.

THE BOYS FROM BOCA

THE BAND was loading its equipment, not one more encore could be squeezed from them, so I headed home. I did not get very far. I did not want to go home. Instead I parked and went for a walk. The night was blast furnace hot and after dancing for hours I craved the cool. In pursuit of a breeze I headed to the docks where narrow board walkways hem the yachts and dinghies. Sure enough, there were soft wisps of scented breeze. Sometimes I hung over the railings hoping to see a torpedo-sized tarpon, or better yet the cement bollard that is the prehistoric manatee.

However, turns out I was not alone. From the other direction came a couple of lads, one lanky, one squat, both in their early twenties, at most. Strolling and chatting, they rolled their rusty banged up bikes on the back wheels.

"Are you lost?" asked Squat, with a smile.

"Not anymore," I replied, and then it was the three of us under a starry night.

After first checking their IDs to make sure I was not leading myself down the garden path to a felony, I offered to act as tour guide. With only an hour before closing we chained the bikes and hustled off. Starting with the clothing optional Garden of Eden, to ogle the naked humans. Here the boys pressed themselves against a wall, overtly traumatized. Product of youth, I surmised. Next stop, to restore their equilibrium was a place where barely clad girls shake it atop a bar. Lanky and Squat imbibed on the mesmerizing angle. Lanky was so hypnotized by the eye-level ass he took a seat at the bar and stared up, as if into the meaning of life.

Meanwhile Squat and I played a game of pool. Squat won. But during our play I learned these lads were from Boca Raton, and I think I noticed Squat winced when he admitted this. Boca had been their parents great idea. Something to do with the need to flee the crime-ridden north, in search of a safe place to raise the cubs. Here were the results; sweet but deeply bored kids.

After the bars closed we found a tiny beach with lounge chairs from whence we counted flying fish firing out the water like shooting stars.

I listened to the boys playfully squabbling over who had landed the greatest catch that day.

"You murdered Skippy?" I was aghast.

"Dolphin, you know, Wahoo. Not porpoises," they assured. "Not Skippy."

By the sounds of things the greatest excitement seems to have been an encounter with a manatee.

"Those things can move!" laughed Squat. "I jumped onto one of them in the harbor and it went totally nuts, spinning like a crocodile! I had to let go!"

Eventually the sun seeped serenely, gracing us with her comely shine. Stinging my tired eyes. I took my leave and driving the one mile to my house I was ready for home. Last I heard the boys wound up in jail.

L.A.R.S.

INSOMNIA CAN be a beautiful thing, provided you don't have any plans. What I love the most is very late at night when the only sounds are the crickets on percussion and the roosters on trombone and the whoosh of passing cars sounding like a snare drum. Then there are the birds, soothingly, at the cusp of day a veritable symphony with trills and peeps. So much is going on yet it's merely the world's ablutions, its waking transformation which in turn shuts me down, quietens the revving, relaxes the nervous system.

The worst thing you can do, as an insomniac, is try to force yourself to go to sleep. However, all this being up all night and sleeping through the day interferes with most social activities, except of course dancing to the fabulous bands at the bars in town. Which reminds me, I had to take a hiatus from the Jail Birds.

I enjoyed the experience far more than I expected. It's been a full year I have faithfully visited the unlucky Ladies in the Monroe County Detention Center. Many faces came and went during that year, some reappeared, others were there since before my first day and continue to sit there, trapped. Candace, the program creator, was very generous in not only inviting me to join her amazing circus, but allowing me to take over in my natural megalomaniac manner. Once a week we all indulged in off the cuff psychotherapy sessions generally leaving us all in tears of laughter. Oftentimes when I arrived I was low on energy but when I left the building both Candace and I and any other volunteers we may have hooked to join us were all filled with buzzing excitement. It was an interesting exchange for everyone involved.

I learned that so many of us feel a natural urge to write down our thoughts and feelings. So many of us are writers. So many of the Ladies wrote impactful stuff with authentic voices all their own, even when they could hardly spell a word, leaning heavily on phonetics mixed with Ebonix. Sometimes making my own dyslexic issues seem pale by comparison so that I felt at times like The Dusty Professor.

So now I arrive at an impasse. I am not inclined to schedules or obligations and one year of weekly anything is my limit. Not to say I shall never return, but the days of regular visits are over. I liked it, I got totally into it, but for now I'm off the charity wagon and back onto my sociopathic concern with myself and the bands and the bars by night and the morning birds. I love their symphonic swells as they greet the day, gradually louder and more vociferous and insistent, some staccato and harsh, some burbling and quibbling sweetly.

The upshot is I am establishing a Large Animal Research Station and I am already at work entering the data from my observations from a year with the Ladies.

ONCE BITTEN

ANOTHER TRIBE worthy of study for the Large Animal Research Station are the Serbians of Key West. The local Serbs move about seemingly in one amoebic glob. They live together, they all mostly work together riding the pedicabs, and they hunt together. You'll see them, peddling the pedicabs, ably hauling soused and sunburned tourists. To look at the Serbs sure are handsome and some are even friendly, but allegedly on nights of a full moon these Serbians are long-fanged otherworldly beasts. Word around town is the Serbs might indeed be werewolves.

For the purpose of observation I made a plan with one of them, my buddy Vuk (pronounced 'voooook'). Vuk agreed to participate in this study and no animals, supernatural or otherwise, were harmed in the compilation of data. Vuk and I forged a plan for the night of the fullest full moon of the year.

As agreed, on that night I met with a cluster of lupine lads at the end of the pier at Higgs Beach. This jetty is a narrow walkway of slats with a banquette at its end, so that you feel you are far out at sea. Here I found them, drinking and laughing, baying, and telling stories. It appeared to me they were all unusually large and dark and exceptionally tall and at times I felt I was standing in an ancient deciduous forest.

"Why would you think we are werewolves?" A redwood asked, handing me a beer.

"I don't!" I said. "But that's what everyone believes. Any ideas?"

Silver jags of light undulated on the ocean's chop, playful and hypnotic. The moon was concealed and then brilliantly revealed through tears in the fast moving clouds. A wind churned to a mini typhoon and it got loud, tangible power.

"You know what Vuk means in Serbian?" An evergreen said. "It means wolf."

I spat up some suds and they laughed at me before someone expounded on the legend of naming a son wolf, so as to scare away the witches who might come to snatch your precious male child.

At exactly midnight Vuk led the way howling at the night sky and we crooned in a pack. It was impossible to dismiss the decidedly were-wolfish traits, and I shivered, though it could have been on account of the gale.

Someone offered, "We're not werewolves. That's ridiculous!" And they laughed at me until I blushed. Scaring me half to death Vuk added, "We're vampires."

I'm not sure anymore what happened but the next day I awoke with a strange mark on my neck and Yeti-sized wet splattered prints on the front porch. Close to a month has passed and besides the still visible trace of a nip on my neck I have yet to regain my equilibrium, my balance is off, and I combust with spontaneous chortling at inappropriate times.

While I track a professional to analyze my findings, (and perhaps bite) I must contemplate the implications. I'll let you know the results.

MEXICAN VACATION

HERE LIES the true story of Swell Merlot, a screenwriter who had run dry of inspiration.

Swell lounged poolside at the Mexican resort, sunbathing in her red bikini. She was supposed to be polishing a script, but she could not focus. Instead she drank and sunbathed and pictured Martin, her boyfriend, on his way to visit her. What she could never have imagined was that at that very moment Martin was hanging from chains in a dungeon. No one could hear his pitiful screams each time his skin was raised in welts from the whip.

Swell was impressed with Martin, he was a decade younger than she, so she cut him slack where normally she might have castrated a dude. She felt he was an artist, undeveloped albeit, who needed time to grow. She thought she understood him. Earlier that day he had phoned, from LAX, "I'm getting on my flight," he had yelled down the crackling line. Swell was excited to see him but it reminded her she should be writing. Swell ordered another drink.

At LAX, with the ticket purchased for him by his tolerant girlfriend, Martin had altered the destination. As his thirtieth birthday loomed Martin had become engorged with the need to do something important. He decided to devote himself to a Mexican guerrilla movement bustling in the south of that enormous country. Story went that he flew down and volunteered himself to the rebels. A little tipsy but laden with gifts of alcohol and an antique musket, Martin had marched through the dusty town, demanding to speak with the rebel leader, known internationally as, 'El Capitan' and had promptly been picked up and tossed into a dungeon.

Martin refused to tell the armed rebels what they wanted to hear so they decided he was probably a spy. They strung him up by the ankles and set about torturing him with a bullwhip. His squeals of wanting only to help their cause made them all the more suspicious. The banditos determined he was a fruitcake and they wanted nothing to do with him. They concluded by deciding he was too stupid to be a spy. They accepted his donations and kicked him out of town.

In tremendous pain Martin made his way north, arriving at Swell's hotel late the following afternoon. She was so relieved to see him that she failed to notice his limp. Later, when she saw the welts on his back she determined the marks were the scratches from some whore's nails, explaining his tardiness, she thought. But he was young, she reminded herself, and she was in love, so she forgave him, no questions asked.

The funny thing is Swell never wrote that script.

WHEN I WAS GWYNETH PALTROW

NEAR THE Main Street of East Hampton, and under lily white tents one hundred authors of varying repute are seated, democratically in alphabetical order, at white clothed snaking tables. Each author sits before their stack of books and a sweeping audience peruse along, stopping to chat with whomever they like, admire, care to know better, and possibly buy a signed and dedicated book or two or three.

Included were Jay McInerney, Nelson de Mille, A.M. Holmes, Clive Davis, Nile Rodgers, Kitty Kelly, yours truly, and Gwyneth Paltrow. Obviously this is about more than mere literature and includes illustrious shiny stars at the top of their game with books on decorating, parenting, party-throwing, baking and vegan clean living.

Due to the inflexibility of the alphabet I had the questionable good fortune to be seated directly beside Gwyneth Paltrow. Since she arrived on the late side I had a chance to make some sales to new and repeat customers. There were hugs and smiles and a bloated sense that all was well.

Then slowly yet unmistakably a line began to form in front of my section of table. These folks were hushed and reverential and had a particularly earnest and focussed demeanor and casting furtive eyes around, clearly single minded and clearly without any interest in yours truly. Unless you count the increasingly urgent question they posed, "Where is Gwyneth?"

I bandied a variety of responses, from, "perhaps you can see she is not here?" Which was met with sullen looks. So I upped the ante and replied by saying, "I am Gwyneth!" This earned me palpably hostile replies of, "No you are not!" Needless to say this only encouraged me and I persisted with more elaborate confections such as, "Yes I am Gwyneth, it's just that I've put on a little weight and gone brunette for a role." This met with nary a titter, instead only dark unsmiling glares.

Then the divinity in question arrived with hubby, children and a couple of massive bodyguards. The worshippers blocked my view of the whole world, abusing my tiny territory upon which to abandon their trash or lean their sorry asses.

So I abandoned my post and took that opportunity to roam the great tent and greet my fellow authors. Which is when I saw the food table, and suddenly I knew what needed doing. I made a plate of miniature sloppy hamburgers, stinky steak sandwiches, and the like and hauled it back to my piece of table.

Gwyneth's bodyguards blocked my re-entry despite my assurance I was a just an author and pointing at my name tag, "No!" they growled, body blocking me. So I was forced to crawl under the table. And there I sat with my meat products, wafting the excellent smells toward my sleek vegan neighbor. She ignored the siren smells of protein. We never did say hello, although I did try to sell my book to her sleek vegan children. No bites.

Dinner, however, at my hosts for the weekend, great friend Anne Hearst and her husband Jay McInerney, which lasted until 6am when a pink light illumined the sky, was a memorably glorious night. I'm already looking forward to doing it all again.

FIGHT

I MADE it back to Key West last night and went directly to my favorite bar The Green Parrot where there was dancing and friends and fun, and then, incredibly, almost a full blown showdown fight with a drunk. In all my time here I've never had any problems at all, despite the fact I'm always out and everyone everywhere is almost always drunk, meanwhile the mood here is mellow. But this man with a floppy hat and a soggy mind decided I had offended him and he got ugly and began screaming threats at me. Thankfully the Parrot is full of very large security fellows and the night's stain got thrown out on his ass, which was mighty satisfying to watch. And then the merriment continued until late. Maybe it was just from being tired, maybe there really was a reason to worry the hothead might pop out from nowhere, but for the first time I felt a little unnerved here in Paradise, and I asked a strapping friend to escort me to my car. Still, it's good to be home.

NO JOKE

LAST NIGHT I went out looking for a laugh. It was long after midnight and as usual I was restless. Soon I was slipping into step with the semi-ambulatory crowd, clumps of drunks moving in algae blooms. Most times I ooze easily, stopping to watch the action or stepping into bars that lure me with music, but not last night. I had a mission, I was hunting Leonard.

The first time I met Leonard I'll confess I did not notice him until he spoke, "Want to hear a joke?" asked a bald man weighing down a flimsy camping stool. He brandished a cardboard sign that read 'Jokes'. "No thanks," I said, and rushed away. Not because I don't like jokes, more of an automatic response. But that was a long time ago and in time I fell into the habit of posting up beside Leonard because to watch him was excellent spectator sport.

Leonard has an unwashed glow, in his worn teeshirt and his jeans shorts with white fringe whiffling around thick scabrous knees, all of him permanently in a coating of sweat. Tied in with the laces of his sneakers is his official license to tell jokes.

The first time I sat with Leonard he worked himself into a state, squirming with embarrassment, he felt it necessary to tell me he was married, and he hoped he was not leading me on. I was shocked and almost sputtered guffaws, almost said, "Is that a joke?" Except there was no reason to insult the man, so I gently explained I was just being a parasite, using him, essentially, for the entertainment value. Since then we have been friends and when I see him I attach like a barnacle.

His work involves flagging down the passersby with tailored speculations on what they might respond to. Leonard is part psychiatrist and he swiftly detects a person's predilections. His jokes come fast, he's funny even when he's corny, and his manner is jovial.

Only once did I see another side of Leonard, when a couple of lads strolled past. They said something I didn't catch to which Leonard went rigid and all of him spiraled into a fury and he spat and hurled insults to their departing backs.

In between interactions with the paying public he ranted at me in intense monologues about his distress with the world. Including a troubling story about the previous joke teller who now languished in prison, presumably for an extended stay. Turns out the man had utterly lost his sense of humor when, arriving home to the sailboat he shared with his girlfriend, he discovered her engaged in some naked acrobatics with a couple of buddies. The man grabbed for his speargun and made a mess of his lady. The buddies escaped and called the police. "Not really funny," Leonard said. "But that's how I got my license."

Last night I was up and down the main street, but no Leonard to be found. Speculation runs rampant.

OX & THE PUSSYCAT

YEARS AGO I lost a friend's Boston Whaler (don't believe the hype) 't the bottom of the Great South Bay, off of Fire Island. I was late to catch the ferry and I recklessly disregarded a brewing storm. Slamming over a bumpy choppy sea I made a slight turn and three medium sized waves filled the little boat, and it vanished. Unlike the movies where you can hang onto a toothpick and bob gracefully to safety, the boat and everything in it were gone in an instant. I was suddenly completely submerged in the cold November water. I struggled to rip off my heavy overcoat and boots, and then I saw my black Persian cat floating past my face, locked in her traveling box. I managed to extract her whereupon she clawed her way onto the top of my head (smart kitty) and slowly we washed up to shore (her fur was a wreck for a long time). The boat was found months later in the reeds, its engines corroded beyond repair, all my possessions were lost, and I missed the ferry that day.

TROUBLED CHILD

YOU CAN tell who isn't going to make it, and oftentimes you are right, but it is still always a shock. A gutting hollowing shock.

When he called you refused to take his call. You became afraid of him. You shrank from him, avoided him, even though you loved him and you felt guilty about doing so, you consciously chose denial.

One time when you pretended to sleep you watched him inch carefully around your bedroom until he found what he had come for, your wallet. He helped himself to all your cash and then he tiptoed away. You didn't have what it took to face the monster. You preferred to pretend to sleep.

You worried each time the calls came in the news would be something atrocious. You always knew it was coming. By not taking the calls you tried to beat fate at its own game.

But of course eventually the news did come. And because fate is a true bastard it was not what you expected, it was worse. How, you think, could it be worse than a lifetime of fears? Impossible. Yet it happened. Worse than your worst fears. Dread that had degraded your own life as much or perhaps more than his.

Now he is dead, just like you always knew he would be. It was just the how of it that was shocking. You were not prepared for a homicide. Everything else, anything else. You had already grieved his demise so often, castigated yourself for its certain eventuality.

Shot in the head. A victim of random crime. That was something you were not prepared for. Could never have saved him from. All your years of blame and weak-kneed concern and intervention were for naught. You could never have prevented this.

The fucking police couldn't prevent this. All they can do is mop up afterwards, notify the next of kin, conduct an investigation.

The call finally came and it thoroughly dismantled you, knocked you over. People will tell you astonishing things, like, "He's in a better place now." Ultimately there is no right thing to say. Everyone is dealing with this in their own debilitated bumbling way.

The death of your child is, well, it's the end like you would never believe.

YO BRIDE

A FRIEND from New York beseeched me to crash a big fancy Cuban wedding at the Casa Marina Hotel last night. And I considered it, but as the time approached I chickened out. Later on, predictably, I was to be found on the dance floor of the Green Parrot, the greatest bar in the history of bars, where a powerful band of Latin brothers from Miami were entertaining.

Gradually I noticed that in amongst the crowd were men in white jackets and ladies in vintage this and that and looking very glamorous, and a bride, all rocking out alongside myself on the tiny sticky dance floor.

The bride begged to be allowed to bust out one song, to which the lead singer replied, a little snarkily, "The bride says she is a professional singer. Well so am I!" He made her wait but then finally acquiesced, calling her up to the stage, with, "Yo Bride!"

She did her thing, an impassioned rendition of Otis Blackwell's 'Fever' and she impressed everyone.

And speaking of chickens...

All of Key West is overrun with chickens. They strut about, force traffic to a full stop so they can do their famously inscrutable crossing of the street. They make noise, they stir up dirt, they shit everywhere and to some people's eye they cast an overall third-world pall. Some people detest the crows of the roosters and I have heard many complain. All they can do is complain because, unbelievably, these birds are protected by local laws. For example, if your dog attacks and harms a chicken you will be heftily fined and your dog will be forced to wear a muzzle. However this being a town settled by pirates and scofflaws some of these birds do meet with unnatural and premature deaths. Also, allegedly, cock fighting organizations visit from Miami and pay poor local children a few bucks to bag some birds.

Personally, I love the sound of the roosters, perhaps because it reminds me of a magical time long ago in the mountains of Colombia. But I have asked the locals, if they hate the fowl so bitterly, why not roast one or two of them? They tell me they do, oh yes, they do a lot of illegal and twisted things to the chickens. I say make pets of these birds.

In Colombia I had a howler monkey for a pet. After returning from a long trip to the States the groundskeeper told me the howler was dead. My suspicion was that the little monkey got eaten, by the groundskeeper. But these things are hard to prove.

CANDACE BUSHNELL WRECKED MY MARRIAGE

IT'S TRUE, Candace Bushnell wrecked my second marriage. Yes, that Candace Bushnell, of Sex & the City fame.

This was a handful of years ago in the wilds of New York City. I was six months into my second marriage when the husband, whose name I cannot recall, declared his intentions on attending a concert, and would I care to join?

I love music, but to me, and my eighteenth century upbringing, a concert is a man on spinet and a lady on harp. As a child, when left alone, I spun Schubert and Tubular Bells. While the second husband loved music as much I our tastes did not mesh. I learned this the first time I attended a concert of his absolute favorite band.

I was dismayed to end up in a muddy field being knocked over by mushroom eaters and drunks lurching around with spilling beakers. A stage was half a mile in the distance with a waving sea of shaggy revelers between me and the tiny dots bouncing and singing. I could barely see the musicians, and the music was like a ribbed ribbon of sound ironed flat and ultimately an indecipherable blur. I did not love the experience.

It was midsummer when the second husband proposed driving to Maine with camping gear and setting up life in a field for a three day marathon of his favorite band. I was a bit horrified. But because this was my second marriage I had learned a trick or two. And one of those tricks is to feign interest in your mate's interests.

While the husbands come and go, friends endure. Candace Bushnell and I have been friends for many years, since long before her well deserved pole vault to fame and fortune. However, when one has friends who publish books, one has to read these books. And it just so happened Candace had recently published her novel 4 Blondes.

Bingo! I was saved.

"Of course, darling," I replied to the second husband. "I'd love nothing better."

Cut to a muddy field in Maine, exterior, day. The outline of the stage was just visible far in the distance, but any hope of seeing anything was made impossible by Bill and Bob Mullet standing right in front of me over whom I could not see. Except I had come prepared.

I plopped down into a cross-legged position and extracted the book and began to read and thus I thoroughly enjoyed myself and believed I had discovered the secret to a happy life. Now and again I peeked up to smile at hubby and I shall confess I did notice a look of derision and contempt on his face. But things were never right again, and in another six months he would be packing and leaving. In retrospect, I believe he considered my behavior sacrilegious, and amongst some other issues, I am fairly certain reading that book was the beginning of the end of that marriage.

Oh well.

OF MICE AND MEN

IN A club after midnight. Men in tight jeans and serious demeanors skulk and track with great intent. Eyes trolling the clusters of young women on towering sculptures and with firm asses encased in micro miniskirts. Everyone clutching drinks. Everyone posing and hunting and overtly behaving covertly. And some of them will get lucky. One couple gets lucky right in front of me, seated nearby on the dark, slightly sticky pleather banquette. She is sitting on him, and they are kissing passionately and with her legs across his lap, neatly crossed at the ankle, one cheek is visible, creeping forth from the hem of the micro skirt.

At four in the morning the lights go on and a small army of bouncers hustle us out.

I walked home down a street lined with trees. At the base of one tree trunk I saw something furry and low to the ground, with a humped rump and skittering movements. And then it plunged headfirst into a hole so that as I strolled past all I could see was a long undulating thick ridged rubbery tail.

TALES FROM THE LAND OF NOD

LAST NIGHT I went to a dinner party, somewhere up the Keys. The liquor flowed and a fresh batch of hash cookies were passed around, (I declined) and then some of the guests volunteered anecdotes.

One lady told about how, and a long night at the house of a friend where they inflicted upon their own persons copious cocaine abuse. At the end of the very long night she swallowed a sleeping pill and laid herself down on her bed to begin to end the raucous soiree, except the sleeping pill had a strange effect and although she did fall asleep she also began to walk around the house. First thing she did was to snort up the remainder of the cocaine and then made her way to the drinks cupboard where she selected some shot glasses, and gave them all a sound telling off, admonishing with a stiff finger, before she threw them out a window.

This prompted a musclebound man with tender watery eyes to admit to a time when he too overdid it with the sleeping pills. As far as he knew, when he awoke with a mild hangover twelve hours later, all was well. Many hours later, feeling just fine, he took his bulldog for a walk, as he's done so many million times before. If not for the doorman's little tale he'd never have known anything untoward had occurred. But apparently, according to the doorman, who spoke with a look of bewilderment and concern, Mr Muscles had ventured out earlier that same day, as per usual to walk the bulldog, except he was looking a 'little strange and sweaty' and was only attired in his boxer shorts. No shirt, no shoes and in the germ and filth riddled streets of the lower east side, and worst of all, allegedly, Mr Muscles and his bulldog were gone for a very long walk. The man look startled and shook his head hard as he finished up telling his story, in a post traumatic stress kind of way.

Another woman told a merry story of sleepwalking, of course completely bare assed naked, into the hallway of a hotel. Where she awoke and had to be creative with a vase to conceal her own self as she was obliged to descend to the lobby and beg for a new key, and all in the buff, save for the vase.

All this served to remind me of a time when I too overdid things with the pills, and in a zombielike condition I began to make phone calls. This was told to me by more than one person long after the fact. Apparently, I had been trying, quite determinedly, to sell a horse farm.

When I got home last night I made a point of forgoing any sort of sleeping pills, and instead nodded off to the dulcet tones of an episode of 'The Bride Wore Blood'. Put me right to sleep.

SPEAKING OF BLOOD ON MY HANDS

I LOVE true crime shows. When I settled down to watch another episode of The Bride Wore Blood and the narrator said 'some of this material might be disturbing to some viewers', I thought, "It bloody well better be disturbing, ha ha!"

Here on the paradisiacal coral rock island that is Key West we have three times the amount of crime than in the rest of the country. Shocking statistics reveal there are three times the aggravated assaults and three times the amount of rapes, almost all of which are perpetrated on tourists, around 4am as they wobble and weave their inebriated selves back to their hotel rooms. For the repeat offender predator these easy pickings are irresistible.

But crime is not restricted to the night or to the obvious miscreants. Recently I went to a doctor and asked for sleeping pills, and he told me to go to a head shop and buy myself a bottle of synthetic pee so as to pass a certain test which would otherwise reveal my recent run in with a joint. I smoked, I explained to the doctor, because it helps me sleep. Obediently I did buy a bottle of 'Urine Luck' but unlike a discreet puff in the confines of my home I have, as of yet, been too timorous to go through with what can only be felonious. While I enjoy visiting the local Federal Penitentiary as a teacher, I'm not so curious to become an inmate.

Florida has a long and florid history, so complex that today the state shaped like a gun is ballistic with contradictions. So, while Florida feeds tourists to the crocodilian predators and bars its citizens from any access to legally produced pharmaceuticals, gun toting is warmly and enthusiastically encouraged.

When my good friend Rhett, musician/mariner/and teller of tales, invited me to the local gun range naturally I said yes please. A couple of islands north we met up at the Big Coppitt Gun Range. Rhett had a bagful of pistols, Wild West style revolvers, riffles and boxes of ammo. With protective glasses and noise blocking headgear, Rhett had to show me exactly how to hold these contraptions, and aim and fire at a poster several feet away down our lane inside the shooting gallery. I was surprised at just how heavy they were to handle, and then the blasted kickback which renders the armament difficult to control. Despite these setbacks it turns out I'm a good shot.

After all the true crime shows I've imbibed on perhaps it's time to join the flow and buy myself a cute little 9mm. If only to brandish at the doctor's office, so as to get a prescription for sleeping pills. And then, who knows, perhaps I'll take over the world.

OFF BASE

CURRENTLY KEY West is bloated from an additional mostly naked 50,000 partiers come to immerse themselves in Fantasy Fest. Including a thirty-something Marine from upstate who drove to town for a single night, to witness for himself the fuss he had only heard of. Despite a couple tours in Iraq and the same again in Afghanistan he was rocked and wide-eyed at the extremes before him. He stopped to photograph a naked lady astride a motorcycle, surrounded by other slack-jawed men also photographing her and a generously displayed glistening poon. The Marine took photographs of himself and porn star Ron Jeremy, who for once had his clothes on. The Marine took many photographs that night, because as he plainly stated, "The guys back home are never going to believe this!"

FANTASY FEST 2013

THE FANTASY Fest migration stampeded in and disrobed and got body painted. Half way through the week the rains came. A flash flood of Noah proportions washing off their eye-popping paint jobs, swirling away into the overpriced and mold ridden gutters that are their rooms for the night. All before last call.

The hot season was a swelter of solid humidity. The air was unbreathable and leaden. Luscious from flowers and fermenting sea grasses sweating on the beaches, and thus ultimately nauseating. Gradually I retreated and spent my days behind drawn blinds, A/C blasting full power, emerging only after sundown.

"Get me outta here!" I complained to my genie. Some have sugar-daddies, others have fairy-godmothers, I have Nalim, the genie.

Today I find the island refreshed with soft breezes, so much so I turn off the A/C and shove open all the windows. Nourishing tropical H2O shuffles through the rooms of my domain.

A malevolent, mischievous genie, that's what I get. My genie lives far away in a bottle up a mountain. He is mostly happy but can get restless, and then malicious.

Twenty-five years ago these same Fantasy Festers came here to git naked and git painted and stroll around. But they looked different. It was hip because they were not the bodies they have today. While it is charming that diehards return and reinvent themselves for the duration of their stay, like temporary insanity, they might consider not removing all their clothes. Just a suggestion, but a quick glance in the mirror will confirm some tits are too awful for primetime. For example, if your nipples are tangled in your belt buckle, put the frittatas away.

I'll admit, between the heat and the breasts I began plotting an escape. Perhaps I absorbed too much recirculating Freon, but after two months of hiding in the A/C and rampant toxic-levels of cabin fever I complained to my genie Nalim, who lives up north somewheres, and he instructed me, "Move to Mississippi! You can buy something for a song. Now's the time."

Nalim, a snake charmer, can cajole me out of my basket of peregrinations and set me robotically upon fresh paths. Instantly, picturing a pale green field and a rainbow dappled farmhouse, I placed a call to a pal in Mississippi, to discuss the purchase of one acre and a mule. Starting small.

Then the weather changed, overnight and my island home filled with fresh air and now town will drain of the energy of those fifty-thousand heat-creating stampeding beasts, in their tutus. The rains dropped from a molten sky. Hot rain. Bathing the coral rock with cool and the hot season was over. My fantasy of Mississippi crystalized and I pictured footage of me in the evenings, too far away from all that I love about Key West and the fantasy evaporated. Just like that. From Fantasy Fest back to reality.

PARROTHEADS

THE PAST few days have been devoted to Parrotheads, the mobile fans of Jimmy Buffett who carbon footprint their way down in pickup-trucks with overinflated tires to the Mecca that is Key West for a celebratory week homage to their hero.

Obviously, Jimmy Buffett is a very clever man, by anyone's standards the dude has made a fortune. But since his product is the musical equivalent of a Trailer Park, and attracts those who dwell in them, his tribe is a shabby lot. Meanwhile, you won't see the likes of Jimmy Buffett in their midsts. A nuance entirely lost on the flock.

Every year a murky rumor drifts through the throngs, "Jimmy Buffett is here!" And so the Chinese whisper gathers momentum. Every year the fans are disappointed, but never disheartened. They come in couples, with matching outfits and they all wear shirts with a parrot motif. Many walk around barefoot because they want to believe they are "in Paradise," just like it says in the song.

Speaking of the songs, the less said the better. I walked all over town and it was an All You Can Eat Jimmy Buffett Buffet. Worse, his fans, whistle with fingers in their mouths at every opportunity, piercing and eardrum shattering. I scurried fast through hallowed halls of entertainment, skittering quickly away from the bouquet of Buffett fans.

I would rather go to jail than spend my Saturday night listening to one more lick. So I did. I paid a visit to the ladies in the local Detention Center. It was a pleasure to see them, plenty new faces to me but some diehards who with luck see glimmers of hope on the horizons of their cases.

There is this one lady who has existed here twenty-two months, defying the state mandate of a maximum one year stay. She is in for murder but the prosecution has no case because there is no evidence. Because, as she tells it, she is innocent. Her waist long straight hair is grey to the shoulder while the tails still hold a memory of gloss, of a luxuriant blonde from two years ago. I saw her eyes well when I secretly passed her a book of stamps. I do not believe she is guilty of murdering her husband. She tells me she might be released no later than February, all charges dropped. Which would sort of prove her innocence. In essence the state is suggesting she is a criminal mastermind of epic proportions who has pulled off 'The Perfect Murder'. A complicated two-step with the penal system.

The creative writing class was a boisterous exchange and soon everyone in the room was falling apart from laughter.

You gotta get arrested in this town to have a good time, some times.

BETTER THAN CAKE

MY FRIEND tells me that on the night of his birthday, which happened to have landed in the middle of Fantasy Fest, he was headed for The Chart Room, one of his favorite bars, for a nightcap. It was late in the evening and he was cruising slowly through the crowd of strangely dressed revelers when he bumped right into a body. A young slender female gorgeously sexy body attired in various black leather straps.

"Great costume!" he said, "Where are you from?"

"Thanks! Wisconsin!" She slurred and she fell into his chest and giggled, "You're cute!"

"It's my birthday!" he said, beaming, up close.

"Happy Birthday!" she responded, and she kissed him. As if it was their last day on earth they went at it. Before very long they were sideways and air humping.

"We should go somewhere," he suggested, adjusting themselves upright.

She stared at him groggily, happily. "Where?"

"There's an alley I know," My friend said, proving chivalry is not dead, and he led her like a saddled pony down a cobbled side street. As soon as they were in relative privacy he bent her over a fence and had his way.

"It was surreal!" he tells me he could hear voices from the main drag. "It was over pretty quickly."

When all was said and done my friend escorted the filly to the end of the alley, and released her back into the wilds of Duval Street.

"I'm so glad I bumped into you," he said to her, and shoved her on her way.

"Cheers!" I said, and clanked my glass against his. Despite a mild case of disgust, like heartburn, I was impressed and happy for my friend, but I had to ask, "Did you offer to walk her to her hotel?"

"Why?" he said, "What if she invited me in!"

However, what I should have asked him was if he put a silver dollar under his pillow to thank the birthday booty fairy.

STRANGER THAN FICTION

WAS IT Mark Twain who said: Truth is stranger than fiction; but it is because Fiction is obliged to keep to possibilities; Truth isn't.

- Well put Mr. Clemens. Some of my strangest stories are true, and so is the following:

A man I know in possession of a great quantity of guns was recently up in front of a local judge. He was there specifically for being wildly drunk at the same time as trying to drive himself home, late one night. Except he never made it because the cops pulled him over, breathalyzed him, determined he was piss drunk and locked him up overnight.

Next the fun began, two years without driving privileges, fines out the ass, lawyers fees out the nose, random drug tests and various privileges curtailed. In order to set sail on a recent voyage to the San Y Islands he was obliged to obtain special permission.

Finally he was scheduled to face a judge to determine the remainder of his situation.

"You've behaved well Mr. X." the judge declared. "Six more months probation and, providing you have no further run ins with the law, you can consider yourself a free man."

"Thank you Your Honor." Mr X said.

"One more question," asked the judge. "Do you have any firearms?"

"Yes, Your Honor. Quite a few. All registered."

"I'm ordering you to turn those over to a Marshall within three days."

"No, Your Honor."

"Are you refusing a direct order of the court?"

"Yes, Your Honor."

"Why?"

"I'm a Southern country boy..." and Mr. X launched into a heartfelt monologue about his rights and exactly how and why he could never be parted from his weapons, working his way up to a tearjerking, "...and I'd sooner die than turn them in."

The judge must have been in a very good mood because all she said was, "OK, Mr Southern Country Boy, you can keep your guns if can you promise me you won't shoot and kill anyone in the next six months?"

"I promise, Your Honor."

A snapshot of Florida's fetishistic relationship with gun owners. Stranger than fiction.

THINGS CHANGE

THINGS CHANGE, and I felt a deep sadness when Darko, my favorite dance partner split town abruptly, and permanently. Life in Key West is an evolutionary experience. Tides swell up the beaches, water nibbling at the sand, plucking and depositing. Very gradually everything is constantly inconsistent. Twirling clouds and twisting topography, and of course the flux of people. Friends I have made have moved on, others are tipping into the beyond. Change is strange and hard to handle especially since it defies time. The big stuff often seemingly happens overnight. Hair turned bright white from fright. I blinked and looked in the mirror and there was a complete stranger looking back at me. Time flying right in my face.

Speaking of Time, one of the Ladies is sprung from the clink but under house arrest. To keep her from crawling the walls I took her beat up broken guitar to be fixed at The Grateful Guitar store on Duval Square where a young man clearly weary from long diligent work hours and burning the ever shorter candle at both ends restrung it and tuned it and generally spiffed up my friend's guitar. The young man did a thorough job so that the instrument shone like new. To check the strings he plucked a lick of classical Spanish and my chi transported. What is it about music?

While I waited, in walked a purple clad music man frequently seen strumming out there on Duval Street, late into the night. His name is Kenyatta and he is a Jimmy Hendrix type, and coincidentally he once knew Jimmy and even played on a couple tracks with the God that was Hendrix.

Kenyatta had with him just the very top part of a guitar neck, he said he had salvaged it after a fight whence a lady be-splattered this guitar on her now ex-boyfriend's head, smashing both blunt objects. The tired guitar fixer said he has heard that story already once this year, and that it's an annual occurrence.

Great sounds last night at the Hogs Breath Saloon with Highway 61 Band and of course The Green Parrot and Xperimento. The music was electrifying and the crowd typically eccentric. One lady wore her King Charles spaniel like a collar, oddly tolerated by the pet. A man danced, taking up every inch of dance floor, and he looked like he was trying to clamber out from a hole in the ground, at great speed. His flailing was riveting and he was obviously having a great time.

At the midnight set break I made my way outside to the sidewalk and was soon happily joined by the very excellent Trombone Player with a beer and a shot for fortification.

I had to ask, "Are musicians ever affected by the crowd? For example a really bad dancer? Could watching someone spasming out ever make you play wrong?"

"Ha, no! But I was wishing I had my camera to take some video of that dude!" the very excellent Trombone Player said, adding, "Sometimes, when we're playing Jazz and people start clapping that can get us all messed up.

Later, a sweet girl in pigtails and dancing shoes asked me to dance. Good times.

The End...

ABOUT CHRISTINA OXENBERG

CHRISTINA OXENBERG was born, and briefly raised, in NewYork City. This was followed by prolonged stays in London, then Madrid, then back to New York before returning to London, and so on, until after fourteen schools and a multitudinous array of stepparents and their tribes of offspring, a precedent for adventure was set. Bypassing University, Oxenberg plunged into a whirlpool of random employment, everything from researcher to party organizer to art dealer to burger flipper. Oxenberg's single true love is writing and she published her first book,TAXI, a collection of anecdotes, in 1986. Despite the lousy pay, Oxenberg published articles in Allure Magazine, The London Sunday Times Magazine, Tattler, Salon.com, Penthouse and anyone else who would have her. In 2000 Oxenberg was seduced by the offer of a regular paycheck and she fell down the rabbit-hole world of fine fibers. In the blink of an eye a decade vanished into an unwieldy wool business. With relief she returns to the relative calm of writing fiction. Between excursions, Oxenberg dwells in Key West, Florida.

Photograph by Leigh Vogel©
www.leighvogel.com

For press, speaking engagements and other inquires contact:

Ox Press
PO Box 1534
Key West Florida 33041

Website: www.wooldomination.com
Email: wooldomination@gmail.com

Made in the USA
Charleston, SC
14 January 2014